A LIVING HERITAGE

A LIVING HERITAGE

St. Stephen's Episcopal Church,
Milledgeville GA 1841-1907

Virginia C. Hinton Ph.D

with research by Janice A. Hardy and editing by
Claire Shepard-Edited with notes by the Rev. Dr.
C.K. Robertson

To order additional copies of this book, contact:
Xlibris Corporation
1-888-795-4274
www.Xlibris.com
Orders@Xlibris.com
21690

✧ CONTENTS

Editor's Preface 7

Introduction 11

1: Beginnings: The 1840s 13

2: The Antebellum Years: The 1850s 26

3: Sherman and the War: The 1860s 37

4: Reconstruction: The 1870s 55

5: Tough Times: The 1880s 76

6: New Challenges: The 1890s 141

7: The End of an Era: The 1900s 193

Appendix 1: Rectors of St. Stephen's 223

Appendix 2: Twentieth-Century Wardens of St. Stephen's 225

Works Cited 229

✧ EDITOR'S PREFACE

Sadly, I had missed it by twelve years!

I am referring to the 1991 sesquicentennial celebrations of St. Stephen's Episcopal Church, Milledgeville, Georgia, marking the 150th anniversary of the organization of the parish by several key laypeople under the auspices of the Rt. Rev. Stephen Elliott, then Bishop of a single Diocese of Georgia. Two years (and much human toil and divine grace) after that seed was planted, the church building itself was completed and consecrated by the bishop as sacred space. Although a 160th anniversary of that event may not carry the weight of an impressive designation such as "sesquicentennial," still it was determined that 2003, the bicentennial year for the city of Milledgeville, should be set aside as a year to reflect on the distinguished and often fascinating history of this building and the people who have worked and worshipped in it. For members of the church, St. Stephen's has endured as a powerful symbol of the living legacy of Christian faith in the Anglican tradition. For residents of this community and visiting tourists, it remains a vital point of interest.

Several significant events were planned for this year of celebration, including visits from former priests and bishops who are part of the heritage of this parish; a monthly series of lectures by local historians focusing on key events and individuals in Milledgeville's story; a quarterly concert series; a bicentennial-themed auction in October; the creation of a Heritage Endowment Fund, incorporating work begun two decades before with the Mae McLaughlin St. Stephen's Foundation; and the addition of a permanent display in the John Garner Room of Warden's Hall for the preservation and display of key parish documents and memorabilia. All this was planned, yet one more thing was needed.

I invited Dr. Virginia Hinton, a retired journalist and mother of long-time parishioner Claire Shepherd, to write a history of St. Stephen's, to be published in December 2003, as part of the rededication of the church by the Rt. Rev. J. Neil Alexander, in remembrance of the consecration in 1843. Virginia focused her attention on the early years of the parish, from its inception to 1907, the year in which the Diocese of Georgia split into two separate dioceses, Georgia and Atlanta, with St. Stephen's incorporated into the latter. The other key person in this enterprise has been retired Georgia College professor Jan Hardy. Doing a grueling amount of "double duty," Jan researched the sources for this book while simultaneously finding articles and resources for a multiple-volume recounting of Methodism in Milledgeville, also published in 2003. Due to the collaborative efforts of Virginia and Jan, *A Living Legacy: The History of St. Stephen's Church 1841 to 1907 and Beyond* was created.

The journey from manuscript to publication is not an easy one, and it is only because of the generous contribution of Dr. Perry and Stella Moore that this book exists. I have no adequate words to express my deep appreciation to the Moores for making this work a reality.

Thanks also go to the Rev. Dr. Harold Lawrence of First United Methodist Church and author of the aforementioned volumes on Methodism.

The crucial, conscientious task of re-typing Virginia Hinton's original manuscript for computer accessibility was accomplished by my wife, Deborah Robertson, to whom I am always so deeply indebted. She was assisted in this task by Beverly Farris and Jennifer Lindenberger.

The original manuscript was intended to serve as a single extended historical record to be added to the church's archives. However, it was also essential to me that a connection be made between the events of that early period in St. Stephen's history and the struggles and triumphs of more recent years. To this end, the book is divided into seven chapters, each reflecting the research done on a particular decade between 1841 and 1907. This material is then supplemented by an extended editorial conclusion to each chapter that shares complementary stories and anecdotes from the years since 1907. In this way, I believe that we have not only honored the heritage of those early years but also the fact that, through so many faithful individuals, the legacy has lived on to the present! Various appendices are likewise included at the end of the book, containing lists and records of key people and events in the ongoing story of St. Stephen's Episcopal Church. To the visionary pioneers and faithful leaders of this parish—past, present, and future—this book is dedicated.

✧ INTRODUCTION

This history of St. Stephen's Episcopal Church has been compiled as a part of the celebration of Milledgeville's bicentennial in 2003. Major sources—including Milledgeville weekly newspapers and various histories of the South, of Georgia, of Milledgeville, and of the Episcopal church in Georgia—have been consulted, as well as the few extant documents from St. Stephen's itself. An early communicant, Mrs. Emma LeConte Furman, "assisted somewhat by the Rector of the Church, J. M. Stoney," wrote on May 1, 1877, as follows:

> It is utterly impossible at the present time, owing to the frequent change of Rectors, and the almost entire passing away since the [Civil] war of the older parishioners, to write anything like an accurate history of St. Stephen's parish." She goes on to cite the lack of "materials save the fragmentary records of the Church and a few scattered and vague reminiscences.

Later in her history, Mrs. Furman repeats, "It is extremely difficult at the distance of time, and with the scanty materials at hand to give any information in regard to the labours or even the names of the early members of the Parish who contributed to the growth and prosperity." She adds that the early names "reappear in every journal of the Conventions as Wardens of the Church." Unfortunately, in neither instance does she give any clue as to the reason for the scarcity of materials.

It is even more unfortunate that the safe at St. Stephen's contains few documents much earlier than the records book in which she wrote her history, though it does contain an electronic copy of a document that appears to be the charter. The records themselves begin with a listing in 1870 of families, baptisms, confirmations, communicants, marriages, burials, and offerings, the latter showing not the donors but the amount, date, and purpose. No Vestry minutes earlier than 1953 survive, and a big gap occurs in those.

In addition to Mrs. Furman's history, various volumes by Dr. James C. Bonner, professor of history at what was then called The Woman's College of Georgia, have provided invaluable information on not only St. Stephen's but the city of Milledgeville and the State of Georgia as well.

Because of the paucity of records at the church, it is gratifying to find numerous accounts in the city's newspapers that document activities at St. Stephen's and, on occasions, those in the Diocese of Georgia. Thus this volume presents a history of St. Stephen's essentially as it was recorded by the town's newspaper. It subsequently provides a partial history of the treatment of St. Stephen's by the town's newspapers, and the treatment does indeed change over time. Some of the items, especially from the early years, are quoted in full to give a flavor of the style in which events were presented to readers of the newspapers.

Nineteenth-century newspapers differed appreciably from those of today; they followed the then current rules for punctuation, capitalization, spelling, and grammatical constructions. Also, as late as the mid-twentieth century, virtually every newspaper had compiled its own style book detailing use of capitals, abbreviations, and so forth. Frequently these did not concur with those in most grammar books. Proof-reading also left a great deal to be desired in many instances.

Items are usually quoted verbatim with a minimum use of the traditional *sic* to indicate an exact quote. For example, the word *Christian* is rarely capitalized. *Church* is almost never capitalized, and the apostrophe is often omitted in *St. Stephen's.*

No effort has been made to identify authors of items quoted and attributed to the editor. Nor have the various editors been identified.

In the typescript copy, sources are given at the end of every paragraph; a source page appears at the conclusion.

1

Beginnings: The 1840s

The famous Anglican poet and preacher John Donne wrote that "No man is an island." Nor is a church. Located on South Wayne Street, St. Stephen's Episcopal Church may appear to be simply one of the many ante-bellum structures in downtown Milledgeville. A brief look at its history, however, provides a much livelier and more interesting perception of St. Stephen's. We enjoy a distinctive past and look forward to an equally challenging future.

Several events highlight our past, but they are so intertwined with the history of the state, county, and city that our beginnings can best be understood within the context of those histories. Further, just as today, the spiritual lives of St. Stephen's parishioners were affected by events in their secular world while they in turn affected histories. Many of St. Stephen's parishioners became community leaders; two governors were communicants, one a senior warden, and an adjutant general frequently served on the vestry and as a lay reader.

The state of Georgia was created in 1732 "as a refuge for European Protestants who suffered injustice at the hand of their overlords." General James Edward Oglethorpe accordingly settled Savannah, on the Atlantic coast in 1733, and made it the first capital of the state. And as one historian puts it, "In a sense, the Episcopal Church in Georgia arrived with the founder." Despite the fact that the Church of England was the established church in the new colony, by 1775 it "found itself in a sorry plight . . . by having few church buildings and even fewer ministers." The Revolutionary War did not help matters (Coleman, 1, 17-18, 55).

For two years after the signing of the Declaration of Independence, Savannah remained free of occupying British troops. It was not until December 23, 1778, that they occupied the capital and caused the seat of government to be moved up the Savannah River to Augusta. The latter then fell into British hands so that "From the end of May 1780 until July 1781, the whereabouts or existence of a state government is uncertain" (Coleman, 81, 85).

Finally, in 1782, when the fighting stopped, "Georgia's state government returned to Savannah." By 1786, the interior portions of the state had become sufficiently important for the Georgia General Assembly to direct the establishment of "a new town, to be called Louisville, to be located within twenty miles of Galphin's Old Town on the Ogeechee as the capital." Thus the state acquired its third capital, approximately 35 miles east of Milledgeville in what is now Jefferson County (Coleman 89, 91).

Although the establishment of the Protestant Episcopal Church of the United States of America is officially dated as October 2, 1789, because of the effects of the Revolutionary War, "in 1790 there was but one active Episcopal Church in Georgia . . . the pioneer parish, Christ Church of Savannah" (Malone, 47).

The next significant date in the history of St. Stephen's is May 11, 1803, when an act of the Georgia Legislature not only created the county of Baldwin but also established a town on the west bank of the Oconee River. It was to be named for the current governor, John Milledge. In December, 1804, the legislature designated the year-old village as the fourth capital of the state (Bonner, *Mill,* 12, 17, 46).

Delays in the construction of the town as well as the building to house the state government prevented its transfer until 1807. Almost immediately the capital, modeled after both Savannah and Washington, D.C., became an important center of commerce, yet it lacked an Episcopal church. This lack can be attributed to mitigating circumstances, which included conditions in the state as well as in Milledgeville. Writing in 1877, an active communicant of St. Stephen's, Mrs. Emma LeConte Furman, points out, "Its frontier position for many years, its sparse population and the apparently firm foothold acquired in advance by the Methodist and Baptist Denominations, all conspired to render the field and unpromising one." The area remained a frontier because much of Middle Georgia was controlled by the Cherokee Indians so that any meaningful foray by the church into the area did not become feasible until their forced removal in 1838-39 (Bonner, *Mill*, 21). Figures bear out Mrs. Furman's appraisal. In 1830, the combined population of the county and town amounted to only 7,250 persons, with slaves comprising 56 percent of the total. Ten years later, Georgia's population was reported by the U.S. Census Bureau as follows:

White males, 210,634	White females, 197,161
Free black males, 1,374	Free black females, 1,379
Male slaves, 139,355	Female slaves, 141,609

Total 691,492 (Bonner, *Mill*, 112-113)

Although white men outnumbered white females, female slaves outnumbered male slaves. Slaves accounted for a little more than 40 percent of the population (White, 43).

The Milledgeville area also lacked any rail transportation, though in 1841 a line was completed from Augusta through Warrenton and Macon. The telegraph did not reach Milledgeville until 1859 (Bonner, *Mill*, 132).

Despite the frontier condition, two priests from Christ Church, Savannah, and the head of the Standing Committee of the Diocese, had held services in Milledgeville as early as 1832. The Rev. Mr. John V. Bartow, rector, and the Rev. Edward Neufville surveyed the frontier territory for seven months, reporting that Milledgeville presented "a field for missionary labor" (Malone, 57; Furman). Indeed, according to Professor Bonner, "A great majority of the people both in the town and in the county remained unchurched throughout the antebellum period" (Malone, 57; Furman, Bonner, *Mill*, 93).

Although three colonial Georgia Episcopal churches had formed the Diocese of Georgia in 1823, it was not until 1840, at its eighteenth annual convention, that the diocese met the requirements for the election of a bishop: six congregations and six rectors (Collins, 5, 12). At Grace Church, Clarkesville, thirty-four-year-old Stephen Elliott, Jr., a native of Beaufort, South Carolina, was unanimously elected the first bishop of Georgia. He put a high priority on the establishment of a church in the state capital, he himself conducting "the first several services in the buildings of Methodist and Presbyterian faiths" (Collines, 5, 12; Bonner, *St. S*; Collins, 19).

Thus, on April 4, 1841, the history of St. Stephen's begins, for on that date, the eighth oldest Episcopal church in the state of Georgia and the third oldest in what is now the Diocese of Atlanta, was incorporated by the state of Georgia. Governor Charles J. McDonald signed the papers, as did William B. Wofford, Speaker of the House of Representatives, and Robert M. Echols, President of the Senate.

On April 19, 1842, a year after the incorporation of St. Stephen's, the wardens and vestry met to begin what must have been a daunting process of erecting a building. The following year, on April 3, 1843, the bishop met with the group and determined the plan for the structure (Furman).

A site posed no problem for the new parish. In the original town plans, one of the public squares had been designated as the location for any church that applied for a one-acre lot. In 1822, however, a new half-acre lot on the west side of Statehouse Square was provided by the legislature. St. Stephen's, the fourth church built on the square and the oldest church building in the city, still stands today on its plot, with the old capitol just up the slope from the back door, literally in the church's back yard. The most recent lease was signed in 1966 for a 99-year-term. As will be seen, the sanctuary's proximity to the state arsenal and magazine, both also only a few yards away, would play an important part in the church's history (Bonner, *Mill*, 24-25).

As with any institution, people make the difference. One of the first to make a difference, in addition to Bishop Elliott, was one of the incorporators, John Ruggles Cotting, the first state geologist. He became senior warden, with the other incorporator, Charles J. Paine becoming junior warden. The remainder of the vestry consisted of Michael J. Kenan, William S. Rockwell, and John Sherrod Thomas (Bonner, *St. S*).

The following year, five new parishes were established in the diocese, including Emmanuel Church in Athens. Together, Emmanuel and St. Stephen's "gave the Church representation in the university center and at the capital of the state. From these strategic places it would become better known to the people of Georgia" (Collins, 22).

The building was constructed in 1843 with a flat roof and without a vestibule and was one of the first consecrated by the new bishop. The service, with the Rev. Rufus White as rector, was duly noted on December 12, 1843, in the *Southern Recorder* (Bonner, *St. S*)

> The Episcopal Church, lately erected in this place, was solemnly dedicated to the Triune God, under the name of St. Stephen's Church, by Bishop Elliot, in the presence of a crowded congregation, on Sunday last. The Rev. Mr. White, late from North Carolina, was installed as pastor. The Rev. Mr. Neufville aided in the service, Rev. Mr. Bragg being also present.

Presumable the latter was the Rev. Seneca Bragg, a native New Yorker called to Christ Church, Macon, where he had served for nearly 14 years (Collins, 20). The news story continues: "The sermon of Bishop Elliot was characterized by his usual vigor of thought and beauty of style."

A mid-twentieth-century historian gives Western New York as the Rev. Mr. White's point of origin and further identifies him as "deacon-in-charge." Mrs. Furman identifies him later as rector. In any event, he served St. Stephen's for two years (Collins, 20).

Unlike twenty-first-century publications, those of the nineteenth century lacked any quick means of communication, including even the relatively simple telegraph, much less sophisticated technology as a news service. News could travel no faster than an individual could. Thus newspapers tended to fill their columns with local news and anything with a so-called local interest. The editor, who usually served as reporter, did not hesitate to add in straight news stories that we would call editorializing. Local stories and obituaries frequently ran much longer than most of those today, especially in larger newspapers. In the days before the advent of the telegraph, newspapers relied heavily upon each other for news. Stories could be copied verbatim because an effective copyright law was still a development of the future.

Just as newspapers lacked modern technology, so did St. Stephen's. It could not turn to the radio or television to inform the people of Milledgeville of its activities. So the papers and the church were dependent upon each other. Certainly Milledgeville newspapers helped keep the name of St. Stephen's before their readers, though the coverage at times seems to have been confined to announcements of service times.

One of the first items, if not the first, concerned pew rentals and appeared in the *Southern Recorder* on December 26, 1843, with no indication as to whether it was a paid advertisement:

> The Pews of St. Stephen's Church, Milledgeville, will be rented for the term of one year, renewable at the pleasure of the holders. Application may be made to the subscriber THIS DAY, and until all are disposed of, who will attend at the Church for that purpose.
>
> J. R. COTTING
> Sec'ry of the Vestry
> Dec. 26, 1843

(Apparently the senior warden was also serving as secretary of the Vestry.) A note of explanation should be made regarding pew rentals. Widely practiced for many years in the Episcopal

Church as a means of financial support, at the founding of St. Stephen's this tradition was likewise followed by the nearby Presbyterian Church, constructed in 1828. Pew rentals continued at St. Stephen's for at least another four years. Once pews became free, notice to that effect was given in virtually every story about scheduled services. One church historian has confirmed that the "practice discouraged the casual visitor and the poor," which might explain one possible reason for the slow growth at St. Stephen's (Collins, 26).

Undoubtedly, the lack of substantial population growth also affected the growth of St. Stephen's. The population of Baldwin County in 1845 had increased to only 7,450 persons: 2,579 white and 4,871 black (White, 133). In May of that year, with seventeen communicants, St. Stephen's hosted the Annual Convention of the Protestant Episcopal Church in Georgia. The following account appeared in the *Southern Recorder* on May 13, under the heading "Episcopal Convention":

> The Convention of the Protestant Episcopal Church, which has been in session here since Thursday last, adjourned yesterday morning. No business of *special* importance came before it. The reports from the different parishes were favorable.
>
> A special ordination was held on Sunday morning in St. Stephen's Church, when the following gentlemen were admitted to the Deacons' orders: Messrs. OWEN P. THACKAREA, NICHOLAS A. OKESON, Wm. J. ELLIS, AND Wm. P. MOWER. The sermon on the occasion was delivered by the Rev. E. E. Ford, D.D. of Augusta, after morning prayer by the Rev. E. Neufville. The candidates were presented by the Rev. Mr. Bragg.
>
> The Rev. Messrs. Neufville, Ford, Bragg and Stevens were appointed Delegates to the General Convention.
>
> The next Convention will be held in Emmanuel Church, Athens, on the Thursday after the first Monday in May next.

The rector of St. Stephen's, however, was "absent in the North, in attendance upon a dying brother, and the newly ordained Deacon, Mr. Mower, a native of Virginia, remained a month or two after the adjournment of the Convention, to supply his place" (Furman). Mrs. Furman continues, "The Rector returned to his charge in the month of October, and in his report to the Convention for the year 1845 mentions that the grounds in front of the church were brought to beautiful order at much expense."

The fourth delegate to the convention, William Bacon Stevens, deserves further mention. He has been described by one historian as "one of the most interesting clergymen in Georgia Episcopal history" (Malone, 74-75). Settling in Savannah to practice medicine, he "helped found the Georgia Historical Society and shortly thereafter began to write a history of Georgia." Bishop Elliot personally trained him for the ministry. Ordained deacon in February, 1843, he was appointed "missionary to Emmanuel Church in Athens," where he became Professor of Oratory and Bells Letters at the University.

No mention is made in the early histories of St. Stephen's regarding its first organ, but records indicate its importance to the parishioners in their worship. Mrs. Furman notes, "From the same source we learn that the ladies of the Parish held a fair in December, the proceeds of which $200 were applied to liquidating the balance still due on the organ, also that the list of Communicants numbered 17." Professor Bonner notes that until "about 1850, nearly all of the church's money raising efforts were devoted to paying the remaining cost of the church organ" and assumes that "this indebtedness in 1845 has been reduced to $200." Some of these efforts took the form of bazaars at the Masonic Hall. The necessity of such means of raising money undoubtedly resulted at least in part from the small size of the congregation (Bonner, *St. S*). Mrs. Furman continues, "We may observe in passing that the Bishop, in his address to the Convention, dwells upon the chaste beauty of the interior of the church," such beauty still evident in the present.

The Rev. Mr. White's resignation on December 11, 1845, left

St. Stephen's without a rector. During his two-year tenure, he baptized 25 persons and presented nine for confirmation (Furman).

In 1846, Sir Charles Lyell, the famous English geologist, included Milledgeville, a "mere village," on is second tour of the United States. One wonders if Milledgeville should not credit one of the founders of St. Stephen's, the state geologist, John Ruggles Cotting, for the visit of such a world-wide famous scientist. For his part, Lyell observed that the building was "neat and substantial" (Bonner, *St. S*).

In July of that year, the Rev. William Johnson became rector with only 11 communicants. Meanwhile, the Sunday school of the church, run by two women teachers, is credited with preserving the church. The Rev. Richard Johnson, steward of the Montpelier Institute in Monroe County, had taken charge of the parish for a few months prior to the arrival of the new rector on July 5, 1846. Mrs. Furman explains that the two priests were brothers (Furman; Collins 78).

According to a letter to St. Stephen's, dated November 14, 2002 (sic), and asking for help with research on St. Peter's Episcopal Church in Lowndes County, Alabama, the Rev. Mr. William Johnson was born near Beaufort, South Carolina, in 1811. He was ordained in his home state, where he also served two parishes. From there in 1840 he went to the church in Alabama, then to St. Stephen's, and later back to South Carolina and, eventually, to Missouri. The letter goes on to explain that his mother-in-law was a member of his household during his Milledgeville tenure. She is identified as Eliza Matilda Lee Love and described as "a very interesting lady of firm opinions . . . a granddaughter of Richard Henry Lee, the signer of the Declaration of Independence.

In 1846, of the 14 communicants at St. Stephen's, only three were men, perhaps one reason for its struggle to survive. Professor Bonner says that the rector "supplemented his eager salary by teaching school, and he also held services at the Georgia Penitentiary for which he received an honorarium" (Collins; Bonner, *St. S*).

Newspaper announcements confirm that bazaars were alive and

well more than 150 years ago. On November 17, 1846, the following appeared in the *Southern Recorder* under the heading "Ladies' Fair":

> The Ladies of the Episcopal Church of this city will hold a fair in the Masonic Hall tomorrow evening (Commencement day,) on which occasion they will exhibit for sale a variety of articles—fancy, ornamental and useful—principally their own handiwork. A fine supper will also be served in the course of the evening. No appeal is deemed necessary to our citizens or the strangers now in the city, beyond the statement that the object to be promoted is the support of religion. Tickets at the door.

Less than a year later, the newspaper ran another announcement of a "Ladies' Fair," also to be held at the Masonic Hall with "a variety of fancy and useful articles' for sale. However, in contrast to the previously announced event, this time a price was quoted: "A fine supper will be served in the course of the evening. Admittance to the exhibition room, 25 cents—children half price. Nov. 2, 1847." The Masonic Hall, with its magnificent spiral stair to the top floor, is located approximately two blocks from St. Stephen's. It still stands, occupied by several businesses.

Readers of the edition of the *Southern Recorder* for February 29, 1848, were assured that an 82-year-old communicant of St. Stephen's, "with a composure rarely exhibited," had "yielded up her life without a struggle." Mrs. Sarah Ann Bugg had died "at the residence of her son-in-law, Thomas N. Hamilton, Athens, Ga., on the 14th inst., at half past 11 o'clock, A.M." ("Inst.," which is frequently quoted, is an abbreviation for the word *instant* and is used to mean "of the current month.) She was described as "full of years, in the perfect possession of her intellect, and not unprepared for the approach of death laboring as she did under a protracted illness of an alarming character, she was well apprised that her days upon earth were but few."

One can hope that Mrs. Bugg's affiliation with St. Stephen's comforted her when, "often speaking of her approaching dissolution, she expressed entire resignation to the Divine will, and to the last declared her trust in the Redeemer. Telling her friends not to weep for her, and blessing her grandchildren, so softly did her spirit pass away, that it was difficult to feel she was gone."

The church was still renting pews in 1848, for on April 18, the *Southern Recorder* printed a small notice under the heading "Episcopal Church," which informed readers, "The pews of the Church will be disposed of as on Monday, the 24th inst., upon application at the Church. Persons wishing to rent will attend at 11 o'clock a.m."

Perhaps, as clergy do today, the Rev. Mr. Johnson also received some monetary token of appreciation for other special services, such as the wedding announced on May 30, 1848, in the *Southern Recorder* in a column headed simply, "MARRIED": "In this city, on the 24th inst., in St. Stephen's Church, by Rev. William Johnson, Rev. EDMUND P. BROWN, Rector of Christ Church, St. Simons, to Miss Susan G. Cotting." She was the daughter of John Ruggles Cotting, St. Stephen's first senior warden and first state geologist.

By 1848, the number of communicants had increased to 17, despite "no change" in the parish, as the Rev. Mr. Johnson reported, "and no promise of better things." However, he continues, "A firm reliance on the power which the Church has by virtue of her diving origin keeps me from despair" (Furman). Regardless of the size of the congregation, he administered "the communion on the first Sunday of every month. Service is performed on Sundays twice and once on each of the principal holy days; also once a week during Lent, and every day in passion week" (Furman).

He was also performing weddings, too. Under the heading "MARRIED", the *Southern Recorder* carried the following announcement on October 8, 1849:

> "On Sunday evening last, in St. Stephen's Church, by the Rev. Mr. Johnson, EZRA DAGGETT, Esq., to Miss CHARLOTTE S. BROWN—both of this city."

The ladies of the church maintained their efforts to raise money, this time with a considerably increased price for their benefactors.

Either out-of-control inflation had set in, or the church's financial status had dropped precipitously. The following announcement appeared on January 29, 1850, in the *Southern Recorder*:

> The Ladies of the Episcopal Church will provide and offer to the public on Thursday Evening next, the 31st, inst., an Elegant Supper, in the Rooms over Mr. Childs' store.
>
> Rooms open at 8 o'clock. Supper at 9.
>
> Price of admission—for Gentleman and Lady, $1— Gentlemen alone, the same.

It truly was to a young man's advantage to take a date!

✠ ✠ ✠

Then and Now: From the beginning of St. Stephen's history, the building itself has been not only a place of worship, but also a vital part of the historic fabric of this city that is regarded with appreciation and respect by non-Episcopalians and church members alike.

Throughout the twentieth century, there has been significant expansion of parish facilities, starting with the creation of what would become known as Harding Hall, named for the Rev. Frederick Harriman Harding, long-standing rector from 1924 to 1954. This space, adjacent to the sanctuary, now holds the offices of the rector, deacon, and church secretary.

In the 1970s, with the full backing of the Rev. Milton Murray, rector from 1964 to 1970, along with the strong support of parishioners Emmett W. Hines and Frederica Boatwright Hines, the parish embarked on the incredible task of constructing the Parish House, now called the Parish Hall. Erected in 1968-69 and dedicated on May 10, 1970, the Hall is a large and beautiful facility with windows on either side, allowing the natural sunshine to flood the room. The main floor of the Hall holds a fully equipped kitchen, as well as rooms that now house the Catherine Cline-Garner Memorial Library, the Virginia Herald Bowman Memorial Choir Room (dedicated on All Saints' Day in 1986, and the Youth Room. An extension was later built onto the main section

*of the Hall, to allow for additional seating or food tables. This extension
was built in thanksgiving for members of the church who served in the
U. S. military. Twice in recent years, the Library has undergone
refurbishment and updating. Similarly, to the Choir Room was added
the Lillian and Wesley Moore Choir Annex for storage of robes and
equipment, and to the kitchen was added an additional pantry for
storage of plates, utensils, linens. The Parish Hall was designed to have
a downstairs section, which was set aside for children's Sunday School
rooms, and would later be the home of the St. Stephen's Day School.*

*Founded by Director Carol Grant with the full backing of the
rector, the Rev. Edward Sellers, the Day School both attracted young
families to the church and also provided an outreach to the larger
community. Today, this award-winning school is well-known for its
quality of care and early education for children age 2 through pre-K,
with a substantial waiting list to which parents often add their children
as soon as they are born! The Day School also serves as a training
facility for students at the John Lounsbury School of Education of the
Georgia College & State University. That same vibrant period of
building and growth that witnessed the birth of the Day School also
resulted in the construction of Warden's Hall.*

*St. Stephen's sanctuary remains an important part of the city tour
for visitors to Milledgeville. In order to preserve the fabric of that spiritual
and historic treasure, the Heritage Endowment Fund was established
in 2003, continuing and enhancing a tradition begun over two decades
before with the Mae McLaughlin Scholarship Fund, also known as the
St. Stephen's Foundation. Following the destruction of a Reconstruction-
era stained glass window during a robbery in early 2003, the first
person to offer funds for the repair of the window was a prominent
member of the city's Jewish community, thereby demonstrating once more
the importance of the legacy of St. Stephen's not only for parishioners
but for all members of the community.*

2

The Antebellum Years: The 1850s

All the efforts of the Rev. Mr. Johnson and those of the women of the church could not prevent a decline in membership to 13 in 1850, perhaps one reason the rector resigned in the last part of the year after a tenure of four and half years. Twenty-seven years later, he was credited with having "laid a foundation which has withstood many vicissitudes, and yet gives its tone to St. Stephen's Congregation" (Furman).

On March 23, 1851, the Rev. Mr. George Macauley became rector. He reported to the convention the next year that the communicants numbered 12. He is quoted as follows:

> This parish has been exceedingly weakened by removals during the past year. The prospect of still greater emigration has had a depressing effect upon those other communions who have for some time been favorably inclined toward the Church, whilst the members who are to remain, conscious of their inability to support the pastor, are impressed with the humbling thought that the Church of their first love is soon to be closed (Furman).

Although the church obviously managed to survive, there was no improvement the next year, and the prospects were described as "very discouraging".

In May, 1853, the church lost one of its oldest members. On

the 31st, the *Southern Recorder* ran the following obituary under the heading "DIED":

> At Scottsboro, in the vicinity of this place, on the 24th inst., after a short illness, Mrs. Abigail Davidson, in the 81st year of her age. During the lifetime of her husband, Capt. John Davidson of Savannah, she was well known in that city, in the polite circles over which she presided, for her unbounded hospitality and suavity of manners.
>
> In later years, though very much confined at home by the inbecilities of age, she greatly endeared herself to all about her, by that uniform kindness which so peculiarly distinguished her. Emphatically the "law of kindness dwelt upon her lips." As a consistent member of the Episcopal Church, her end was peace—"To die was gain."

On November 8, 1853, the paper ran a long paragraph on Episcopal appointments, with the explanation, "We copy, and adopt as our own, the following from the *Savannah Republican* of the 28th. The remarks relative to Mr. SCOTT are especially appropriate and true, and we readily and cheerfully endorse them."

There follows the account of the appointment of the Rev. Thomas F. Scott, of Columbus, Ga., as "Episcopal Bishop of Oregon, and the Rev. Dr. Kip of Albany, N.Y., Bishop of California—Dr. Kip is the author of several works on religious topics, and Mr. Scott is known in this State as one of the ablest divines and warmest friends of education that we have."

The January 24, 1854 edition carried a long paragraph from the *Savannah Journal* on the consecration in Savannah of the Rev. Mr. Scott as a Missionary Bishop:

> The ceremony was solemnly and impressively performed in accordance with the regular established Church form. The officiating Bishops were the Rt. Rev. Stephen Elliott, Bishop

of Georgia, and pastor of Christ Church, who presided, and the Rt. Rev. Bishop Cobbs of Alabama, and the Rt. Rev. Bishop Davis of South Carolina.

Other clergy participating in the service were also listed.

"In 1854," according to Mrs. Furman, "the skies seem brightening—the number of communicants has increased to eighteen and the parish appears slowly but steadily growing." She made no mention of a "Sabbath School Celebration" that the *Southern Recorder* reported on July 11 of that year:

> The different Sunday Schools in this place held a celebration on Saturday last, which was very numerously attended. Addresses of the boys were delivered in good style. [Author's note: Did only boys attended, and if so why? If girls were included, why were no addresses given by them?] They were followed by the Rev. Mr. Daniel, of the Baptist church, an able and impressive address to parents. The children were briefly and appropriately addressed by the Rev. Mr. McCauley, of the Episcopal church. The large audience, comprised of the Sabbath school teachers and scholars and spectators, then formed a procession and proceeded to the State House where a very bountiful repast awaited their arrival. The exercises of the occasion were enlivened at the church with appropriate odes. The Milledgeville Brass Band also kindly tendered their services. Altogether, the occasion was one of deep interest and, we trust, will awaken more lively solicitude on behalf of the Sabbath School cause.

On October 24, 1854, the *Southern Recorder* devoted several inches to the obituary of a Milledgeville native living in Savannah, where she had become a "devoted member of the Episcopal Church." The account begins, "Few persons among the victims of the recent pestilence in Savannah, have died more lamented than MRS. MARY ANN RYAN." The obituary continues: "Although Mrs. Ryan had not been a year in Savannah at the time of her death, she had made for herself many friends who valued her for her understanding and loved her for her virtues." The account explains that "During the summer of 1853, Mrs. Ryan made a public profession of religion, and was baptized in Christ Church, Savannah, by the Rt. Rev. Bishop Elliott. She was afterwards confirmed." Growing up in Milledgeville, she later lived in Sandersville, "where she was well known as a successful and valued teacher. She is affectionately remembered and sincerely lamented in both places by a large circle of friends. Her example is all that is now left to them and to her children."

Evidently the bishop's activities merited attention, regardless of where they took place. On May 22, 1855, the *Southern Recorder* reprinted from the *Marietta Georgian* the following:

BISHOP ELLIOTT AT MARIETTA.—The Rt. Rev. Bishop Elliott has passed the week in this city. He is one of the most eminent theologians in the country, an ornament to the Church, a thorough scholar, and a gentleman of whom our State may well be proud. He officiated at the confirmation of a large number, last Sabbath, and his discourses on that day, and during the week, were listened to by appreciating audiences.

After five and a half years, the Rev. Mr. Macauley resigned, so that St. Stephen's lacked a rector until November 1, 1857. Although Mrs. Furman's account says he left on October 14, 1856, the *Southern Recorder* reported on December 16 that he performed at least one marriage, that of "Mr. Robt. N. Adams and Miss Martha J. Wooten, all of this city." The Rev. Marion McAllister of St. Mary's volunteered his service for two or three months, as did a visitor to Milledgeville, one Dr. Maybin. The *Southern Recorder* reported on June 16, 1857, under the "MARRIED" column, "In this city, on Sunday night, June 14th, at St. Stephen's Church, by Rev. Dr. Maybin, MR. ROBT.N.ADAMS and Miss MARTHA J.

WOOTEN, all of this city." However, since he had not been "regularly called," upon the advice of the bishop, he left (Furman). The Rev. Dr. Carmichael, the next rector, is identified only as having come from the Diocese of Western New York. Bishop Elliott observed in his address in 1858 that Dr. Carmichael was reviving the church. The rector reported that "communion Alms were kept for the purchase for a suitable Communion Service" (Furman).

On April 13, 1858, the *Southern Recorder* reported that "THE RIGHT REVEREND BISHOP ELLIOTT will preach and administer the rite of Confirmation, in the Episcopal Church of Milledgeville, on Wednesday or Thursday next; of the particular time of holding the service, due notice will be given after the Bishop's arrival."

The next month, on May 18, the newspaper gave the following account of the beginnings of one of the Church's preeminent universities:

> EPISCOPAL CONVENTION—The annual Episcopal Convention of Georgia assembled in Savannah on the 6th inst. The Bishop's report refers to the project for building a Southern Episcopal College, under the patronage of the Church, which is to rival anything in this country in its capacity and usefulness. The location selected in Sewanee, Tenn., and no work to be commenced until $500,000 is collected, only the interest of which is to be expended—the principal to be retained by the treasurer of each State.

On June 28, the *Southern Recorder* carried the following paragraph:

> Bishop Polk has succeeded in getting ten gentlemen of his diocese in the Episcopal Church to subscribe $300,000 towards the establishment of the great Southern University. One old gentleman—formerly U.S. Senator, and subsequently Governor of Louisiana, the Hon. Mr. Johnson—has subscribed $40,000 to the University.

Two years later, on October 10, 1860, the cornerstone for the University of the South was laid (Malone, 92). The Rt. Rev. Leonidas Polk, bishop of Louisiana, has been called "a unique general . . . a brave and noble gentleman." Educated at West Point, he resigned his commission to enter "the Virginia Theological Seminary in 1861, accepted a commission in the Confederate army and no longer exercised his episcopal authority" (Eaton, 112-13; Encyclopedia Britannica, vol. 18, 168).

Appointed a major general in October, 1862, "he was promoted lieutenant general" and given a command of one of the three corps of the army of Tennessee." He was killed on June 14, 1864, on Pine Mountain, northeast of Marietta, Georgia, and his body lay in state in either St. James Episcopal Church in Marietta or a nearby grove (WBH, Jr.).

Meanwhile, after less than a year, the Rev. Dr. Carmichael left St. Stephen's in August 1858. However, the *Tri-Weekly Recorder* on November 27, 1858, tacked a postscript on the bottom of a report of Thanksgiving Discourse, held on the previous Thursday. The editor began, "There was no service in any of the churches in this city on Thursday last." He added a sentence at the end: "P.S. Since writing the above, we learn that there was a service in the Episcopal Church." No clue is given as to who conducted it.

This time the parish did not lack a rector very long. On January 1, 1859, the Rev. Judson M. Curtis assumed the duties. His coming had been duly noted in the *Southern Recorder* on December 21, 1858, under the heading "EPISCOPAL CHURCH":

> The Rev. J. M. Curtis, of Hopkinsville, Kentucky, having accepted a call to the Rectorship of St. Stephen's Parish, there will be regular services at the Episcopal Church, in this city, commencing on Sunday, January 3d, 1859, at 10 o'clock, A.M.

His tenure was marked by the construction of the first rectory. He reported to Convention in 1859, "We have a small neat cottage nearly completed. It will cost $1200" (Furman).

The parish regrettably continued to suffer from emigration, though no causes are given. The Rev. Mr. Curtis reported eleven confirmations in 1860, but the number of communicants was listed as only twenty-one.

✠ ✠ ✠

Then & Now: The tradition of the parish supplying a rectory for the rector has given way in more recent years to providing a housing allowance for the purchase of the rector's own home. The last rector to live in a church-supplied rectory was the Rev. Jay McLaughlin. The Rev. Milton Murray, rector of St. Stephen's from 1964 to 1970, has alluded to the tornado that crashed through the downtown rectory, situated across the street from what is now Georgia College & State University. In a welcome note to his later successor, the Rev. Dr. C. K. Robertson, Fr. Murray offered his wish "that you will be very happy here in Milledgeville" . . . then adding, "and I hope that your house never gets hit by a tornado!"

The children's Sunday School program—termed "Sabbath School" in those early years of the parish—has enjoyed both rich times and struggles in the twentieth and twenty-first centuries. Frances Thornton relates Jack's description of the scene in 1927-29, when he was young:

Miss Mattie Thomas was the teacher and there were only four students in the church: Jack, 10; his brother Steve, 13; Frances Hines and Harriet Campbell, both probably about 15. The class was held in the church with the four on one pew and Miss Thomas sitting on a pew three rows in front of them. He hated it and when he got to be 13 and put on long pants he went to the Presbyterian Church, where there were a lot of boys his age. The class was taught by Erwin Sibley and [Jack] still has a letter written by Mr. Sibley congratulating him for a perfect attendance.

Amie Hodges (then Amie Jennings, the wife of Harry Jennings, who worked on the Union-Recorder when the editor was Jere Moore) started the Sunday School and found the room was about as big as a large closet with a table, and assembled around the table the few students (all ages) were each given a pamphlet and told to read it. That was it! Amie knew something had to be done . . . so she started. She set up some card tables in the aisles of the church and got others to help and had different teachers for different ages. Mr. Frank Bone (who was Senior Warden as long as he lived) came to church early on Sunday and was appalled at the idea. So he had a small room added to the back of the church which Amie said immediately was taken over by the choir; they would throw their robes on the Sunday School tables. Later, another room was added where [the parish secretary's] office is now. In the fall of 1945, when Jack returned from service in Europe, I brought Jack, Jr., then 2 years old, to Sunday School, and helped Amie for many years. Carolyn Rotter (now Carolyn Herne) and Inez Hawkins and others helped. Another helper was a second grade teacher at Peabody, Mary Beth Busby, who later married Fr. Bill Kirkland. . . .

Another teacher was Eleanor Wade who taught her daughter Martha, Claudia Davis, and my son Dennis and others that age for a number of years; they all loved her. (Those three students were born in 1947, so these classes were held in the 1950s.) I remember she held a summer class some years later and made my youngest son Steve acolyte when he was about four, and there he was in his little white robe and bare-footed. She said he was her "little angel."

I can also remember when Jere Moore was the Superintendent, all students would be assembled in the sanctuary for a roll call. He always called my son Dennis Turner, my father's name. One time when, all people, Mr. Margiovecco (who taught Spanish at the college) was elected superintendent. Evelyn Stallings' youngest child George talked sort of funny and she wondered if . . . he would need to go to a special school. So she asked Mr. Margiovecco to observe him and see what he thought. So Amie and I had

these four year olds sitting around a table coloring. Mr. M.
sat down by George and peered over his head. George
immediately got up and went to the other side of the table
with Mr. M, following. George said, "Got the biddes (sic)
nose I ever saw!" And only Amie and I understood what he
had said and had a hard time suppressing our laughter.

The big event each year for the children was the
Christmas pageant. One year we got some big sheets of
cardboard and gave them to the children and told them to
draw something for the manger scene. I remember Dennis,
who had some artistic talent, drew a big donkey and a lamb,
and Carol [Thornton, now Grant] an angel. The other
children [drew] the three wise men and some others [drew]
animals. One year Amie got Jack to put a light bulb on the
back side of the rail to the sanctuary and each chld in turn
would kneel there; Jack in the background would turn on
the light and it would give the appearance of a halo on the
child's head. One year Jim Bonner asked if he could read a
Christmas story; we were delighted at the idea and gave our
consent. Imagine our surprise when he got up and read,
"How the Grinch Stole Christmas." Another Christmas,
Amie had somebody put a platform across the choir seats
and the girls were on the left side dressed like angels and the
boys on the right as shepherds.

*Throughout the latter half of the 1900s, the story of the Sunday School
could be described as "hit or miss." When lay leaders such as Amie
Hodges have arisen to organize, teach, or assist in the program, the
results have been very exciting. Praise has already been given to the Day
School program, founded by the Thornton's own daughter Carol, which
in its early years was a significant draw for parents of young children.*

*Other programs, such as Vacation Bible School, have enjoyed great
success at times, thanks to the efforts of many faithful parishioners, and
the establishment of the Jake Heindel Memorial Children's Chapel,
complete with beautiful stained glass windows created by artist/teacher
Cathy Wood, has allowed opportunities for children to enjoy their own*

version of the Liturgy of the Word. In recent years, adult volunteers too numerous to count—but including Sharon Stewart, Amelia Pelton, Cindy Gilbert, Debbie Robertson, Susan Reddick, Kathy McGee, Beth Gamble, Mike Martino, Bev Farris, Kelly Shadwell, Cathy Wood, Risa Allen—have provided different avenues of fun, fellowship, and learning for our children, through Easter Egg Hunts and Halloween Carnivals.

The Thorntons speak also of the vital role played by the Acolyte Program in the earlier years of the twentieth century:

> When my boys were young all three of them were acolytes, as were Alling Jones, Frank and Tom Hines, Harry Jennings, Frank Davis and others I can't think of now . . . Now I would like to make this point: They were all boys, no girls. I think the first girl acolyte I remember was Anne Marie Ethier, then Carolyn Galli, then Rebecca Grant.

The Acolyte program has in recent years become an active group even outside the church services, with social events and training sessions. It has benefited greatly from the leadership of people such as long-time Acolyte Mother Kathy McGee; former acolyte and Eagle Scout Joe Simmons; former acolyte, Lay Reader, and Choir member Alling Jones; and Deacon Alice Fay. With well over two dozen acolytes in the program, the group has now participated in events such as the Diocesan Acolyte Festival in Atlanta and the National Acolyte Festival in Washington, D.C.

Clergy and laity alike have long wanted positive outlets for our youth, and faithful volunteer youth workers have arisen through the years to make a difference in the lives of our middle and high schoolers. Whether it was Jack and Marianne Joris or, more recently, Kelly Shadwell, these lay youth leaders have given both time and energy. In more recent years, the Vestry voted to establish a paid part-time Director of Youth Ministries position, and the result has been very positive. Angela Garrett (now married to Roger Otero and living in Augusta), Pat Steed, and Mandy Hodges have helped create Bible studies and fellowship gatherings that attract our youth, and their friends outside St. Stephen's. Diocesan events such as Happening and New Beginnings and parachurch ministries such as Young Life have helped broaden the description of parish youth ministry. Many people hope that the future might hold a similar movement from the model of a purely volunteer children's ministry to the creation of a paid position of Director of Children's Ministries. Until that time, St. Stephen's continues to struggle with needs not altogether different from those faced a century before.

3

Sherman and the War: The 1860s

The weather in the Milledgeville area on January 1, 1861, presaged what lay ahead for St. Stephen's, for Milledgeville, and indeed for the entire country. A young female resident, Miss Anna Maria Green, whose father was the first superintendent of the Georgia Lunatic Asylum in Milledgeville, recorded in her journal: "It has rained almost incessantly the greater part of today, and has been cold and disagreeable out of doors" (8).

Two days later, after a two-year tenure, the Rev. Mr. Curtis left St. Stephen's for a charge in Arkansas. His departure was "greatly lamented" by the people, who "made strong efforts to retain him." Bishop Elliott remarked to the convention in 1861 that his resignation "is very much to be regretted, for he was truly valued and beloved among us" (Furman).

The wardens reported for that year that the communicants numbered twenty-four. Gen. Henry C. Wayne, adjutant general of the state of Georgia and often a member of the Vestry, continued to be a lay reader. Also, "the Holy Communion was occasionally celebrated by the Rev. Mr. [Henry K.] Rees of Christ Church, Macon" (Furman).

Other events in 1861 proved more momentous for St. Stephen's than the loss of a rector. Within a two-month period, the parishioners of St. Stephen's found themselves citizens of three different nations and before the year's end, members of another national church organization.

Following the re-election of President Abraham Lincoln in 1860, South Carolina led the secession of southern states on Dec.

20, followed by Mississippi, Florida, and Alabama. On January 16, 1861, a convention called by Gov. Joseph E. Brown met in Milledgeville. Described as "the most distinguished group of Georgians who had ever assembled in the state," the convention voted on January 19, 1861, to secede from the union. Whether St. Stephen's joined in the celebration, which included the ringing of church bells, is not recorded. Regardless, the church found itself located in an independent republic rather than the United States (Coleman, 151; Bonner, *Ga Story,* 283; Bonner, *Mill,* 156).

On February 4, Georgia delegates met with those from other seceding states in Montgomery, Alabama, and formed a new nation, the Confederate States of America. Georgian Alexander H. Stephens, a native of what is now Taliaferro County, and an 1832 graduate of the University of Georgia, was named vice president (Morris, 228-29; Britannica, vol. 21, 386-67). Two months later, on April 13, the Civil War began with the surrender of Fort Sumter to South Carolina forces.

Bishop Elliott, expecting the state to secede, had already suggested that in such an event prayers for the U. S. President should be changed to "thy Servant, the Governor of the State of Georgia" (Malone, 94). Georgia's bishop was one of three to recommend a convention of Confederate dioceses to "consult upon such matters as may have arisen out of the changes in our civil affairs." The bishops carefully noted that neither ecclesiastical dissension nor doctrinal differences were involved. The resulting Protestant Episcopal Church of the Confederate States was formed, with the constitution being adopted at a meeting in Columbia, South Carolina, in October, 1861, and approved by the Diocese of Georgia later that year (Malone, 94, 98).

Up until this time the Episcopal Church had not been torn asunder by the slavery question, unlike both the Methodist and Baptist Churches. The former had created "a separate Methodist Episcopal Church, South," in 1845. The controversy "led to a similar schism" among American Baptists the same year and the formation of the Southern Baptist Convention in Augusta (Coleman, 181).

The short history of the Confederate Episcopal Church began with Bishop William Meade of Virginia as senior prelate. His death on March 14, 1862, left Bishop Elliott as leader. The other senior bishop, the Right Reverend Leonidas Polk of Louisiana, was serving as a general in the Confederate Army. The church managed only one General Council, in 1862, in Augusta. Canons and by-laws that differed from those of the national church only in details were adopted (Malone, 94-95).

One of Bishop Elliott's first actions involved St. Stephen's: The appointment of the Rev. Mr. Samuel J. Pinkerton of Darien as "General Missionary for the Diocese," responsible for parishes unable to fill vacancies. St. Stephen's was one of those parishes, and it was the one the Rev. Mr. Pinkerton chose as his headquarters during the early years of the war. Announced as "rector pro-tem," he "met with the vestry which included John S. Thomas as Senior Warden who have replaced William S. Rockwell" (Malone, 102; Bonner, *St. S*). "Others were Howard Tinsley, Boswell de Graffenreid, Richard M. Orme, Jr., John M. Clark, and William H. Scott." Richard Orme's father owned the *Southern Recorder*, possibly one reason for the amount of publicity the church received in the newspaper (Bonner, *St. S*). Other priests temporarily served, with General Wayne acting at times as lay reader.

Mrs. Furman's history attributes the parish's lack of a rector to "the political excitement which ensued" and the fact that "all interests were absorbed in the impending war." By March 862, the United States Navy had taken control of Georgia's coast. Yet for part of the year 1863 the parish enjoyed a "flourishing life," which an influx of refugees helped produce. Some of them came from the coastal region, some from North Georgia "in anticipation of Sherman's destructive campaign in that region" (Coleman, 198; Bonner, *St. S*).

The following letter, on a single folded sheet of paper which had then been folded again, was found in one of the record books in the safe at St. Stephen's. It was not enclosed in an envelope, and no reference to it has been located. At this point it is impossible to determine whether it was ever mailed or how it came to be preserved in the record book. Although it gives no clue as to the identity of the addressee, it does provide insight into the devotion of Georgia's adjutant general and the officers of St. Stephen's at a critical time in the state's history:

Milledgeville, February 9, 1863

My dear General.

The Vestry of St. Stephens have had a meeting and adopted the following preamble and Subscription list 'Whereas the Church of St. Stephens in Milledgeville being now free from debt, and as parishioners believing it to be our duty to St. Stephen's, to the Church at large, as Churchmen, and to Almighty God as Christians, that we should make an effort to obtain the Services of a Settled clergyman and the regular administration of the rites and sacraments of the church (in connexion with another Parish) we hereby pledge ourselves to the Vestry of St. Stephens to pay in quarterly installments at the rate per annum opposite our means, leaving the Church settings free.'

"Our subscription here will amount to at least six hundred dollars. It already amounts to four hundred and forty, and not one third of our parishioners have been called upon.

"I am therefore authorized by the Vestry of St. Stephens to propose to the Vestry of the Church of the Advent Madison, a connexion until such time in the future as our means will warrant other arrangements. Our plan proposed is this. You can raise your pay two hundred dollars. The Bishop tells me there is an annual missionary fund for Madison especially of two hundred and fifty dollars. This will make a fund for Madison of four hundred and fifty dollars. Now we suggest that a clergyman by employed to serve the two parishes at an income of one thousand dollars a year, and traveling expenses. We are to give six hundred to salary. The fifty of yours overplus, and a sum to be made up here to go to the traveling expenses. Will you call your Vestry together and respond to our proposition? And appoint a committee for arranging the terms definitely between the parishes. At the same time, if you think fit, intimate your choice of a clergyman, or authorize your committee to bear with us on that point. We can do something if we make the effort, and the right sort of a man will I think build up our churches under Gods blessing. Put your shoulder to the wheel my dear general. Small sums paid quarterly are more easily collected than large ones annually, and by having seats free an inducement is afford to many to attend church. Let me hear from you as soon as convenient.

With [illegible] and wife Maggie
Yrs Truly, Henry C. Wayne

Extant records show that during part of 1863, the Rev. Charles W. Thomas served as a missionary, but in April, the bishop reported to the convention that Dr. Ridley had accepted the call to St. Stephen's. Mrs. Furman does not give his full name but reports that he began the first Sunday after Easter with a congregation nearly double that of the preceding year—forty parishioners in all—many of them refugees. These "came from the coastal region of Georgia and South Carolina. There were also a number of new residents who had come from North Georgia in anticipation of Sherman's destructive campaign in that region" (Bonner, St. S.).

The refugees, along with "the influx of people as a result of legislative sessions and other state business conducted at the seat of government," created a scarcity of food and resulted in hunger for many families (Bonner, St. S).

Although Milledgeville's first experience with "the realities of invasion" did not occur until the summer of 1864, the town experienced almost as much hunger and privation during the war as it did in the period which followed" (Bonner, Mill, 117, 162). Professor Bonner has written, "During the first of April when the suffering had reached catastrophic proportions, St. Stephen's announced its Passion Week services with daily morning and evening prayers (Bonner, *St. S*):

> On April 10, 1863, during Good Friday services, a hungry mob of citizens broke into stores and warehouses in Milledgeville and pillaged them for food and other scarce commodities which they carried off by the armful.
>
> The local police watched the scene in utter helplessness. Later local officials were unwilling or unable to make arrests and to bring the rioters to trial. As a result a detachment of state militia was dispatched to the scene by Governor Brown with orders to arrest the offenders.

The following year, 1864, the number of communicants at St. Stephen's swelled to 60, but Dr. Ridley resigned to join the faculty of Montpelier Institute. Any baptisms thereafter were presumably performed by the bishop and the Rev. Mr. Rees. Two Confederate Army chaplains stationed in the area, the Rev. Mr. Telfair Hodgson and the Rev. Mr. J. M. Schwar, also performed "services as they could, from the summer of 1864 until probably the spring of 1865" (Furman).

Meanwhile in the summer of 1864 a roving band of Union cavalrymen under Gen. George Stoneman struck southward from Atlanta and threatened the capital. Before his capture at Sunshine Church "near Clinton on July 27, he had set in motion plans for a raid on Milledgeville" (Bonner, *Mill*, 177).

Governor Brown learned of the plans and called out enough troops to avert any "physical damage to the capital," though it suffered a "great psychological blow. Throughout the entire period the town was filled with wild rumors, exaggerated stores, and deep apprehension" (Bonner, *Mill*, 178).

General Sherman began his march from Atlanta on the morning of November 15, 1864. Part of what happened three days later, on November 18, as he approached the capital, was recorded by young Miss Green who was still keeping her journal. She described the scene at the State House as "truly ridiculous, the members were badly scared" (Britannnica, vol. 1, 763, 60).

The Georgia Department of Natural Resources, Division of State Parks, Historical Sites & Monuments gives the following account of the lengths to which state officials (and their wives) went to thwart the invaders. A plaque erected on the corner of the square in front of the old Baldwin County Courthouse contains the following information:

> Within 500 feet east of here lived Georgia's wartime secretary of state, Nathan C. Barrett. At midnight, November 18, 1864, just before the arrival of the Federal Army, he and his wife Mary, buried the Great Seal under the house. His wife hid the unfinished acts of the Legislature under the pig pen. These, with the Great Seal, were returned unharmed to the State Legislature at Macon in February, 1865.

Before the army could reach Milledgeville, the legislature adjourned so that members could flee and escape capture and probably imprisonment. The governor, however, who had already removed as many of the state's records as possible as well as the money in the treasury, "remained in the capital an entire day after it was abandoned by the legislature and most of the Statehouse officials" (Cook, 54; Bonner, *Mill*, 196).

Professor Bonner seems to agree with an account that he quotes from the *Southern Confederate* that the governor worked "diligently to safeguard the state's property. Then he boarded the last train out of Milledgeville and accompanied his family to Montezuma," ultimately going to Macon, where he assembled the legislature (Booner, *Mill*, 196). The account continues:

> The most publicized event involving the governor's hasty exit was recorded in a story that he had gone to the vegetable garden and pulled up all the collards and cabbage to take with him," a story that persisted despite his explanation that the cook had gathered the vegetables.

The capital was left undefended because General Wayne had moved the garrison. In effect, when the Union troops occupied Milledgeville, not a shot was fired by either side (Bonner, *Mill,* 182).

Sunday, November 20, the day that the vanguard of General Sherman's army entered Milledgeville, has been described as "a day of unprecedented excitement in the capital of Georgia." It had taken the Army only five days to march from Atlanta to Milledgeville (Bonner, *Sherman,* 273).

That afternoon cannon fire could be heard to the west of town. The first small group of Union soldiers actually to enter the capital "advanced cautiously through the streets with cocked pistols and carbines. They cut telegraph wires, seized a few horses, and then made a hurried exit." In the four days that followed, "more than thirty thousand enemy soldiers entered Milledgeville" (Bonner, *Sherman,* 273).

The fact that a cold rain began late that first day and continued the following day may account in part for some of the destruction the invaders caused. They arrived, "cold, wet, and mud-caked." On the night of November 21, the temperature dropped below freezing "under a biting raw wind. It was the coldest November weather in the memory of most natives" (Bonner, *Mill,* 183). As a result, "picket fences and outhouses became the principal supply of firewood for 30,000 soldiers . . . Church buildings provided greater protection from the cold than army tents—and church pews made excellent fuel—so all church buildings and their contents suffered some damage" (Bonner, *Mill,* 183). St. Stephen's was not spared. Its "organ was ruined when sorghum molasses was poured into the pipes" (Bonner, *Mill,* 183).

General Sherman himself rode into Milledgeville on the morning of November 23, with the main body of the Northern army. In his memoirs, written some 10 years later, he described "the first stage of the journey" as "complete, and absolutely successful," quite a different interpretation from that recorded the following month by the editor of the *Southern Recorder.* The general also remembered that "the people of Milledgeville remained at home, except the Governor (Brown), the State officers, and legislature" (663-64). According to the general, they had "ignominiously fled, in the utmost disorder and confusion, standing not on the order of their going, but going at once—some by rail, some by carriages, and many on foot" (664). Sherman occupied the governor's mansion, which he found "stripped of carpets, curtains, and furniture of all sorts. The items removed by Governor Brown included "even the cabbages and vegetables from his kitchen and cellar" (664). As a result of the governor's prudence, the general "was forced to sleep on an improvised bed and to use a table made from boards placed across camp chairs." To the general's credit, the governor, upon returning, found little evidence of the general's occupancy (Bonner, *Sherman*, 281).

Such was not the case with the capitol when "some of the younger officers staged a mock session of the legislature." Soon soldiers appeared and wrecked the entire building, "including the state library located on the ground floor. Most of the books were thrown out of the windows to the muddy ground" (Bonner, *Sherman*, 284).

All this vandalism was taking place in virtually the backyard of St. Stephen's, though General Sherman offers a different version of what happened:

> Some of the officers (in the spirit of mischief) gathered together in the vacant hall of Representatives, elected a Speaker, and constituted themselves the Legislature of the State of Georgia! A proposition was made to repeal the ordinance of secession, which was well debated, and resulted in its repeal by a fair vote! I was not present at these frolics, but heard of them at the time and enjoyed the joke (660).

Fortunately, during the occupation, "Only three or four private residences in the vicinity of the town were burned," and the "Oconee Mill, the textile factory, and the foundry all escaped destruction, probably because their owners were Northerners or men of foreign birth. Sherman honored almost every excuse for not applying the torch, and even accepted worthless bonds." One of the houses spared belonged to the wife of the editor of one of the newspapers quoted in this account, the *Southern Recorder*, Mrs. Richard M. Ormer, Sr., originally from Andover, Massachusetts (Bonner, *Mill*, 187; *Sherman*, 281).

Because of its location near the state arsenal and magazine, St. Stephen's suffered more loss than that of the organ when occupying troops burned the arsenal and used dynamite to explode the fireproof magazine. All the church buildings on the Capitol Square suffered to some extent, but St. Stephen's the most. The roof was damaged and all the windows shattered (Bonner, *Sherman*, 283).

A single day in the capital sufficed for the general. According to his memoirs, "On the 24th we renewed the march." He did not comment that it was Thanksgiving Day, "although the occasion was foodless and devoid of festivities." By the next day, Milledgeville was no longer occupied by General Sherman's army (Sherman, 667; Bonner, *Sherman*, 287).

Concerning the day that the army left, Miss Green wrote, "This morning the last of the vandals left our city and burned the bridge after them . . . But we were despondent, our heads bowed and our hearts crushed—the Yankees in possession of Milledgeville. The Yankee flag waved from the Capitol . . . Our degradation was bitter, but we knew it could not be long, and we never desponded, our trust was still strong" (63).

Clearly she was far too optimistic concerning the future, for "farms and plantations which lay on the route followed by the army appear to have suffered greater pillage and devastation than the town itself" (Bonner, *Mill*, 188).

The editor of the other Milledgeville paper, the *Confederate Union*, gave the following description: "A stillness almost Sabbath like pervades our business streets, and the blackened walls of the Penitentiary, Arsenal, Magazine, and Depot remind us constantly of the presence of the vandal hordes of Sherman" (Bonner, *Sherman*, 288). He also reported private papers and public documents filling the streets and squares, especially around the statehouse, where window lights were missing and plastering damaged.

Professor Bonner has commented, "The material damage to the community was of little importance in comparison to the wanton destruction of food, livestock, and provisions of all kinds. There was very little left to eat either in the town or in the surrounding countryside after the three-day visit of thirty thousand men and half as many animals to a community of less than four thousand inhabitants" (Bonner, *Sherman*, 289).

What did other members of the occupying army think of Georgia's capital? Most of the soldiers were too cold or too busy washing mud from their garments to write. One surveyed the arsenal, the contents of which he considered of little value against the more modern arms available to the Union troops. One of the officers, however, "was impressed with the old aristocratic atmosphere" did not feed the hungry citizens of the community. The women of St. Stephen's did their part to help the needy, holding suppers to help raise funds. They were particularly concerned about the children and their education (Bonner, *Sherman*, 287; *St. S*).

It was not until about a month after the occupation that the *Southern Recorder* was able to resume publication. On December 20, 1864, under the heading "THE YANKEES IN MILLEDGEVILLE," it was reported:

> The Yankee visitation has prevented the publication of this paper for several weeks. We resume publication to-day under unusual embarrassments, rising from the absence of the junior editor, who shouldered his gun on the advance of the enemy and is still in the militia, perhaps in Savannah, and also from the Yankee impressment of our negro pressmen. In addition to this we have scarcely any mail facilities and have seen of late papers from abroad only through the courtesy of friends, who have loaned them to us. Hence it was worse than useless to have issued the paper, had we been able to print it, when it would not have left Milledgeville.

(By "abroad," he meant simply papers from elsewhere in the area, not from overseas.)

Miss Green was not the only person with illusions about what was happening. The next column in the *Southern Recorder*, under the heading "Sherman's Run," gives an equally mistaken appraisal, one which undoubtedly would have afforded the general some amusement:

> Although Gen. Sherman has damaged us greatly in our Railroads and private losses, still it is incontestibly proved that it was not a triumphant march, but a retreat to avoid starvation at Atlanta, he being cut off from his supplies by Gen. Hood. In confirmation of this, he studiously avoided fighting and turned aside from places where there was the least resistance. He would have gone round Milledgeville in like manner, as one of the Federal Major Generals said, if our soldiers had remained here.

The editor, in the column on "THE YANKEES IN MILLEDGEVILLE," also announced, "To bring up our history of the past, we republish our letter to the Macon Federate Telegraph written two days after Sherman left this city. This letter is a summary of events. Time has not only confirmed those facts, but revealed still greater desolations."

His account did not mention St. Stephen's by name but did record that "the Churches were entered and materially damaged."

Meanwhile, General Sherman was continuing his March to the Sea, during which "the destruction and pillaging continued. With all of Georgia under Federal control, General Sherman moved north on February 1, 1865, into South Carolina. In April Jefferson Davis fled Richmond and held the last meeting of his government in Washington, Wilkes County, Georgia. On April 9, Gen. Robert E. Lee surrendered to Gen. Ulysses S. Grant. Five days later, on April 14, President Abraham Lincoln was shot, dying on April 15. Virtually all the Confederate forces ended their resistance by the end of May (Coleman 203-04; Morris 245).

In a space of about four years, the parishioners of St. Stephen's had belonged to three different nations: the United States, the Republic of Georgia, and the Confederate States of America. To whom did they belong now? That question was not answered definitively for another three years. Georgians thought that action of the Legislature, still meeting in Milledgeville, in December would restore the state "to the Union without further ado. Such was not to be." The Thirty-ninth Congress of the United States was meeting in Washington at the same time, but with far different notions, notions that resulted in the disastrous Reconstruction measures (Coleman, 209). It was not until the Omnibus Act, passed by the U.S. Congress in June, 1868, that Georgia—along with Arkansas, Alabama, Florida, Louisiana, and North and South Carolina—was readmitted to the Union (Morris, 248).

In contrast, re-admittance to the National Church presented no difficulties. Bishop Elliott did not attend General Convention in October, 1865, so as "not to embarrass its utterances or its action." He was delighted to report to Georgia Episcopalians that "instead of anathemas" coming from General Convention, "there were warm greetings of renewed friendship and tears of reconciled love—instead of excommunications, there was hearty welcome and assurances of rejoicing hearts over the healing of the wounds which had been produced by political strife." At the final meeting of the General Council of the Confederate States of America, it was decided that each diocese should make its decision as to returning to the National Church. Georgia joined other dioceses in 1866 in the reunion (Malone, 108-09).

Meanwhile, from Easter Monday, 1864, until January 15, 1867, St. Stephen's struggled to survive without a rector. From late 1865 to 1868, an Episcopalian, Charles J. Jenkins, served as governor and as senior warden to St. Stephen's. His executive secretary, William H. Scott, another Episcopalian, served as junior warden (Bonner, *St. S*).

On January 15, 1867, according to Mrs. Furman's history, the Rev. Benjamin Johnson took charge. St. Stephen's was counted among the 22 contributing parishes in the diocese that year and was assessed $50 for the Bishop's salary for the coming ecclesiastical year (Malone, 110).

Mrs. Furman acclaimed the year 1867 as "probably the most

prosperous one financially and numerically in the history of St. Stephen's parish. The Seaboard refugees still remaining gave a large list of Communicants and Gov. Jenkins' residing here added the full weight of his influences to the other causes of the Church's prosperity—nevertheless, Mr. Johnson reported: 'No baptisms or Confirmations have taken place this year.'"

The next year St. Stephen's suffered two losses, the first being that of the rector. As a result of his resignation early in 1868, the Standing Committee made the church's report to convention; the number of communicants had fallen to 36. Mrs. Furman's history continues:

> This Convention year also marks the death of Bishop Elliott, who was buried on Christmas Day, 1866 (;) while the loss of this great and good prelate was deeply felt not only by the whole Diocese, but also throughout the Church at large, this parish had a peculiar right to lament the man who under God had been its early Father and Sustainer, and whose fostering hand had oft-times upheld its feeble life when all but threatened with extinction. The Record of his life—his death—of his intellect and of his labours for Christ are all fitly preserved elsewhere. Yet it is meet that the history of the parish which owes so much to his zeal and care, should also add its tribute to his memory, in chronicling the death of its benefactor.

Another church historian writes that the bishop apparently "had been in bad health for some months," but when questioned, passed it off as "only weariness." The Rt. Rev. Stephen Elliott died on December 21, 1866, in Savannah (Malone, 108).

Thus, the election of a new bishop became the main order of business at the forty-fifth Annual Convention in May 1867. On the eleventh, two candidates were nominated: the Rev. John W. Beckwith, rector of Trinity Church, New Orleans, and the Rt. Rev. Thomas F. Scott, Missionary Bishop of Oregon, formerly pioneer rector of St. James, Marietta. The former was elected by a vote of more than two-to-one. Beckwith was consecrated on April 2, 1868 (Malone 114-15). Whereas the first diocesan bishop had been a native of South Carolina, the second was born in Raleigh, North Carolina in 1831. A graduate of Trinity College in Hartford, Connecticut in 1852, he served parishes in his home state and in Maryland before becoming a chaplain in the Confederate Army (Malone 116).

Meanwhile, in Washington, D.C., on May 29, 1865, President Andrew Johnson announced his plan for reconstruction, and on June 17 named James Johnson from Columbus as Governor of Georgia. In the November general election, voters replaced Johnson with Charles J. Jenkins of Richmond County, described as a "man of scholarly attainments and dignified bearing" (Coleman 208-09).

Despite the prosperity that St. Stephen's enjoyed in 1867, in March of that year "a new chain of events destined to change drastically the course of the town's history had begun." The change was set in motion "when Congress inaugurated its plan of military reconstruction," setting aside the president's plan (Bonner, *Mill,* 215). Georgia was made part of the Third Military District, with General John Pope in command. He arrived in Atlanta on April 1 and began military occupation and control of the state. General Pope ordered a convention to be held to draw up a new constitution, replacing the constitution of 1865. The convention was to meet, not in the capital city of Milledgeville, but in Atlanta. This resulted in "the hammer blow to Milledgeville's pride and her dignity as the state capital." It came "suddenly when a simple clause providing for the removal of the capital to Atlanta was inserted into the new constitution" (Bonner, *Mill,* 220).

In January 1868, General Pope was succeeded by General George H. Meade. The former's rigor has been cited as the cause of his removal: It did not "suit the Johnson men in Washington as well as in Georgia, who pressed the President to remove him." Unfortunately, "General Meade's popularity was speedily nipped in the bud when he removed Governor Jenkins and other state officers." He sent Brigadier General Thomas H. Ruger to become provisional governor of Georgia. Thus, the state acquired another

Episcopalian as governor. The last of "the Milledgeville governors" remained in office until July 4. His "many acts of kindness" were acknowledged in a set of resolutions from the local citizens (Coleman 212; Thompson 162-63; Bonner, *St. S*). Meanwhile, Governor Jenkins had "attempted to prevent military authorities from plundering the state treasury." He also hid both the state seal and the executive seal. One account says he took "the great seal of the state and about $400,000 in state funds" to New York because he questioned the legality of some of the Reconstruction Acts. Professor Bonner says "the Reconstruction program . . . left in its wake a dreadful spiritless hangover unlike anything which the war had wrought" (Bonner, *Mill*, 227).

Despite efforts to bring the capitol back to Milledgeville, the new one was officially opened in January 1869, in Atlanta . . . and there it remained, in a town that "was enjoying a bustling growth and prosperity which few Georgians had ever imagined." Milledgeville, on the other hand, "remained unchanged, and her friends felt that they were custodians of the Old South and its finest traditions." So it was that Georgia became the only state in the old Confederacy to move her capitol as a result of the Civil War and subsequent Reconstruction (Bonner, *Mill*, 229; *Sherman*, 291).

Records show no further involvement by St. Stephen's in state politics. The church continued without a rector from the resignation of the Rev. Mr. Johnson in 1868 until January 1870, when the Rev. Mr. John Philson was called. He "remained not longer than five months," according to Mrs. Furman.

One of Philson's pastoral duties may have been the funeral of Mrs. William H. Scott, wife of a former vestryman, reported in the Southern Recorder on April 19, 1870. She was identified as a member of the Episcopal Church, but St. Stephen's was not mentioned.

During his short tenure, the rector participated in community activities. The Southern Recorder's printed a lengthy account on May 3 of the observance of Memorial Day on April 26, still observed in Georgia in 2003 as Confederate Memorial Day. The "last and beautiful benediction" came "from the lips of the Rev. Mr. Philson, Rector of St. Stephens Episcopal Church of this city."

Two weeks later, on May 17, the Southern Recorder reported on the Protestant Episcopal Convention, quoting from the annual report of Committees on the State of the Church. A "very considerable increase in the growth of the Church in Georgia, during the past year" was revealed. The account showed 647 baptisms, 274 confirmations, and 2,880 communicants, with total offerings amounting to $87,484.51. The piece concludes:

> We call attention to the total offerings, as it exhibits a united and Christian liberality, such as is seldom manifested. The average contribution by the membership was $30.39. The highest total offering before the war was only about $25,000.

Evidently the state was beginning to recover from its ravages.

Mrs. Furman relates that the Rev. Henry E. Lucas, also in charge of Ascension Church in Sparta, replaced the Rev. Mr. Philson. Dr. Bonner says the Rev. Mr. John Tuken also served as rector during this general time period, but no specific dates are given. (Bonner, *St. S*) The Federal Union supplies some sketchy information. On October 4, 1870, the local column, under "Religious Notice," says, "We are requested to state that services will be held at St. Stephens (Episcopal) church in this city on next Sabbath by the Rev. Mr. Leacock."

✠ ✠ ✠

Then & Now: No event has so marked the church, as well as the city and state, as much as the Civil War (or, as several refer to it, the War of Northern Aggression). Newcomers and tour groups alike hear the tale of "Sherman's stables," the blowing up of the flat church roof when the arsenal was detonated, and the unfortunate incident of molasses poured down the pipes of the organ. There is, of course, a delightful ending to that last tale.

It begins with the fact that it was a New York regiment that allegedly did the pouring. In the early years of the twentieth century, a young girl named NYLIC—her name an acronym for "New York Life Insurance Company," for whom her father worked—wrote a letter to the president of the company, telling of the dastardly deed done half a century before by New Yorkers, asked if it might be possible for the company to make amends and actually purchase a new organ. Amazingly, a Western Union telegram was sent back to Nylic from the president of the N.Y.L.I.C., with the simple message: "Buy the organ and send me the bill." Later still in the early 1990s, as the sesquicentennial of the parish approached, the Rev. Edward Sellers and lay leaders wrote the insurance company yet again, this time requesting the purchase on behalf of St. Stephen's of an original painting of the historic church building by the well-known regional artist, Stan Strickland. The response from New York was, again, a Yes, and the original painting (from which many copies were made and sold to parishioners) still hangs in the parish office. It should be noted that, for that happy celebration, the Union-Recorder ran a delightful picture of Fr. Sellers and choir member Marietta Thompson riding onto the front lawn on horseback, a reminder of days gone by. So, despite the sad events of the Civil War years, St. Stephen's has happily found some recompense for our losses of a century-and-a-half past.

St. Stephen's is indeed an antebellum church that has survived the Civil War and more besides. Through events such as the 2003 Bicentennial Lecture Series on the History of Milledgeville, ongoing trolley tours that include a visit to the church, and the establishment of a permanent display of documents such as the aforementioned Western Union telegram, the memories of those unpleasant days in the 1860s will forever remain a part of our living heritage.

4

Reconstruction: The 1870s

Regardless of whether St. Stephen's had a rector, the Southern
Recorder for April 18, 1871, reported that the bishop would be
present when the Macon convocation would "meet at St. Stephens
Church . . . on Friday morning next, April 21ˢᵗ, and continue
through Saturday." Further, he would "administer the rite of
confirmation on Sunday 23ʳᵈ" Now the church was emphasizing
that "the pews . . . are free and all are invited to attend."
Furthermore, "morning and evening services" would be held on
"Friday and Saturday at 10½ A.M. and 7½ P. M." Virtually the
same notice ran that day in the Federal Union.

The Southern Recorder reported the following week that
"Bishop Beckwith has been in our city for several days. He officiated
at St. Stephen's on Sabbath, performed the rite of confirmation,
and preached in his usual elegant and forcible style to an overflowing
congregation." On the same day, the Federal Union also ran a
paragraph with the same information.

In July, St. Stephen's lost another communicant who had
played a prominent part in the political life of the city and state,
Capt. Lewis H. Kenan, Secretary of the Senate of Georgia, Senator
of this district, and Mayor of Milledgeville, Civil War veteran. He
was said to be about 38 years old. Although the actual cause of his
death is not stated, the editor included in his lengthy obituary on
July 12, 1871, a resounding condemnation of "the growing
tendency of the age, among our people, to right their wrongs with

their own right arms instead of appealing to the law." Readers were informed as follows:

> The funeral of Capt. Lewis Kenan took place from the residence of his brother, Dr. T. H. Kenan, on Wednesday morning inst. The services were conducted by Rev. Mr. Jarrell of the Methodist Church and Rev. Mr. Johnson, of the Episcopal Church, formerly pastor of St. Stephen's Church in this city. Business was very generally suspended and the people turned out en masse to pay the last sad tribute of respect to the departed . . . After the impressive burial service of the Episcopal Church, the Good Templars formed around the grave and said, "There is rest for the having weary."
>
> He was eulogized as having possessed . . . many of the qualities of his late lamented and gifted father, Col. A. H. Kenan. Nature and education had lavished their gifts upon him, making him a most genial and fascinating companion and a polished gentleman. Warm-hearted, fearless, and unflinching supporter of what he thought right—impatient of opposition, jealous of his honor, quick to resent an injury, but magnanimous and forgiving—a true friend, a dangerous foe—a genuine type of Southern chivalry and the spirit of the age.

Another lengthy piece, "In Memoriam," lamenting the young man's death from "the Telegraph & Messenger of the 6th," is reprinted immediately below the obituary.

In 1871, the parish finances had recovered sufficiently for repairs on the building to be completed. The Southern Recorder surely expressed the feelings of St. Stephen's parishioners when it reported the following on July 18, 1871:

> Improvement—We were glad to see on Monday last, workmen employed in making much needed repairs upon the Episcopal Church. The building was badly damaged

by the explosion of the Arsenal in the vicinity, during the
occupation of the city by Sherman's army.

The editor is no longer calling the occupation a "visitation."
The late bishop's name still warranted notice. On July 19, the Federal
Union reported, "Rev. Robert Elliott, son of the late Bishop Elliott, has
been called to the care of St. Philip's Episcopal church of Atlanta."
    In the absence of a rector, a supply priest is always welcome.
The same newspaper, on August 23, notified readers, "The Rev.
Wm. C. Hunter of the Church of the Atonement, Augusta, will
hold services and preach in Episcopal Church (St. Stephens) in
this place on Sunday next, 27th inst."
    The editor of the Recorder must have been keeping up with
the repairs reported in July, for on August 29 the paper informed
its readers, "PLEASANT—St. Stephen's Church looked beautifully
(sic) last Sunday, with its new coat of plaster—paint and varnish."
    The paragraph below revealed that another supply priest had
visited St. Stephen's, "Rev. Mr. Duncan of Augusta," who "delivered
two sermons, and administered the communion to the congregation
of St. Stephen's last Sunday."
    On January 24, 1872, in its church directory, the Federal
Union noted that St. Stephen's was "without a Pastor at present,"
though Sunday school was still meeting at 9 a.m.
    How well received would be Bishop Beckwith's Lenten pastoral
letter, printed in its entirety in the Southern Recorder on Fenruary
27, 1872, especially regarding the reading of novels and attendance
at theaters: "Finally, brethren, I urge you to abstain from all theatres,
balls, private parties, mere ornamental pursuits unnecessary
delicacies."
    Regardless of whether the church had a rector, vestry elections
had to be held. The one for 1892 was reported in the same words
in both the Southern Recorder on April 2 and in the Federal Union
on April 3, 1872:

> At a meeting of the congregation of St. Stephens Church
> held on Easter Monday, Colonel John S. Thomas and Dr.

James W. Herty were elected Senior and Junior Wardens, and Fleming G. Grieve, John M. Clark, Bernard R. Herty, Farish C. Furman, Thomas H. Kenan and John Wilcox Vestrymen.

The Vestry elected Fleming G. Grieve, John S. Thomas and James W. Herty as delegates and John M. Clark, Farish C. Furman and Thomas H. Kenan as alternates to represent the Church and Parish in the next convention of the Diocese to assemble at Columbus, Georgia, 8th May next.

The laity was apparently maintaining the Sunday school, for The "Order of Exercises for Memorial Day," in the Southern Recorder for April 23, listed St. Stephen's as fifth in the procession.

Yet another visiting priest was announced on September 11, 1872, in the Union & Recorder under "Religious Notice": "Rev. George N. James Will hold service and preach in St. Stephen's (Episcopal) Church next Sunday."

News of one of the worst fires ever to strike Milledgeville, a conflagration that killed one man and did damage estimated at a hundred thousand dollars, was reported in the November 27 edition. It threatened not only St. Stephen's, but also the Presbyterian and Methodist churches. "About half past three o'clock on Friday morning 22d inst.," the Union & Recorder recounted, "the citizens of Milledgeville were aroused from their slumbers by the alarm of fire."

Apparently it first awakened "some of the boarders at the Milledgeville Hotel." A headline over one section of the story seems slightly misleading:

THE CHURCHES ON FIRE—The sky was dark and threatening, and while the roof of the hotel was burning the wind was high, blowing from the north-west, sending the sparks upon the churches. The roofs of the Presbyterian, Methodist and Episcopal churches were each on fire at different times, but were promptly extinguished.

On December 11, readers were told "Rev. J. W. Beckwith, Bishop of the Diocese, is expected here next Sunday. He will preach and confirm a number of candidates in St. Stephen's Church." There follows the usual reminder, "Pews Free." The follow-up on the bishop's visit was printed on the 18th: "All the pulpits in the city were filled on last Sabbath. Bishop Beckwith preached at the Episcopal Church." The same story contained the news that "The Episcopalians have secured the services of Rev. Mr. Lucas of Athens as their pastor for next year."

Mrs. Furman's history continues, without mentioning the fire or the amount of damage it did to the roof of St. Stephen's:

> Second Sunday in Advent, 1872, the Parish had now probably reached lowest point in its descending scale since the War, and its strength numerically was as in 1861-twenty-six communicants-the wave of refugees having entirely receded and passed away.
>
> From this time the prospects of the Church grew more encouraging. Through the efforts of the younger people of the parish $280 was now raised and expended in repairing the Church, which had been damaged by time and the explosion of a powder magazine by the Federal Troops.

The Milledgeville Union and Recorder included in its Church Directory on March 5, 1873, the following announcement: "Hours of services on Sunday—11 o'clock, a. m. and 8 p. m. Sunday School 3 p.m. Evening Prayer Wednesday 4 pm." It is signed by the "Rev. H. E. LUCAS, Pastor." Elsewhere in that edition, the entire pastoral letter of Bishop Beckwith was printed. Issued from the Episcopal residence in Savannah on Ash Wednesday, February 26, 1873, it contains no reference to any topical events in either the Church or the state.

The same announcement of services at St. Stephen's as had appeared on March 5 was reprinted on April 2, again signed by "Rev. H. E. LUCAS, Pastor." However, that issue also included among its "Religious Items" the following paragraph: "We learn that Rev. Mr. Lucas of St. Stephen's Church in this city, has resigned the pastorate of that Church, and will return to Athens." According to Mrs. Furman, he did not announce his resignation until April 15.

Under the heading "St. Stephen's Church," readers were advised on April 23 that the vestry election had been held as usual, on Easter Monday:

> Col. John S. Thomas was elected Senior Warden, Dr. James W, Herty, Junior Warden, and John M. Clark, Fleming G. Grieve, Farish C. Furman, Thomas H. Kenan, Bernard R. Herty, John W. Wilcox and Frank B. Mapp, Vestrymen . . . Dr. James W. Herty, Fleming G. Grieve and John W. Wilcox were elected as delegates and John M, Clark and Farish C. Furman as alternates to represent the Church and parish in the Convention of the Diocese shortly to assemble at Savannah.

The paper was "pleased to announce" on June 4, 1873, "that Rev. H. E. Lucas, late Rector of the Episcopal Church of this place, will be with us again this week and hold service in the Church next Sunday at 10½ o'clock. "During the short stay of Mr. Lucas among us, he won the hearts of our people and was especially beloved by his immediate charge."

St. Stephen's was fortunate that a new rector would soon assume his duties at the church, for the Union & Recorder reported on September 3, 1873:

> The community will be pleased to learn that St. Stephens Church in this place is again to be opened for regular services. The Rev. J. M. Stoney of Savannah, recently ordained by Bishop Beckwith, has accepted a call to the Parish, and will enter upon his ministerial charge on the first Sunday in September. We bespeak for Mr. Stoney a cordial welcome and substantial support from our hospitable and generous community."

One of his first duties was to help host a convocation, notice of which was given in the Union and Recorder on October 8 and repeated on the 15th: "A Convocation of the Episcopal Church, with the Rev. W. H. Clark, (Dean), presiding, will be held in this city, opening on the 21ˢᵗ inst," the agenda following.

Also in that issue, an announcement quite unlike any news story today appeared under the headline "Usages of the Episcopal Church":

> After the adjournment of the Convention (to meet here on the 21st inst., a notice of which appears elsewhere) Addresses will be delivered on the evening of the 23d inst., (Thursday,) at 7 o'clock, P.M., in the Senate Chamber in this city, setting forth the claims and usages of the Protestant Episcopal Church. A general attendance of the public will evince, it is hoped, a proper interest in this important subject, and is respectfully requested. Rev. Mr. Drysdale of Athens and Rev, Mr. Kramer of Augusta, will be present; and one or both of these gentlemen, perhaps others also, will address the public. Remember, the evening of the 23d.

The following week, the paper reported, "The Convocation of Episcopal clergymen in this city last week, gave our citizens an opportunity to enjoy a series of interesting services at St. Stephen's Church. The following ministers were in attendance, viz: Rev. Messrs, Clark, Drysdale, Kramer, Reese and Lucas."

On November 19, the paper reported the marriage "On Thursday, 13th inst. at St. Stephen's Church, in this city, by Rev. J. M. Stoney, the Rector, Capt. W. W. Williamson to Miss Kate Clifford Kenan, daughter of Capt. M. J. Kenan. All of this city."

In an almost unreadable paragraph on December 3, the Union & Recorder called attention to services at St. Stephen's at 11 a.m., and 4 p.m. that day, which had been "appointed . . . as a day of intercession to Almighty God on behalf of the mission of the church throughout the world."

Either few newsworthy events were occurring, or the bishop

remained important enough for the Union & Recorder to print on February 25, 1874 the entire pastoral letter of Bishop Beckwith, which says in essence the same things as the ones of 1872 and 1873. He quotes St. Bernard, "If the appetite alone has sinned, let it alone fast, and it sufficient; but if the other members also have sinned why should not they suffer?" Further on, he quotes St. Chrysostom, "What advantage is it if we have kept the fast without mending our morals?" He further admonishes, as he had previously, "For your own good, and for the sake of your example, abstain from worldly amusements, such as theatres, balls, private parties, novel reading, etc."

Two items appeared under the heading "Church Services" on March 18, the first reporting, "Rev. Mr. Stoney conducted the usual services at the Episcopal Church last Sabbath." Also, "Bishop Beckwith will visit our city Wednesday the 18th inst., and will confirm a Class in St. Stephen's Church at 7 o'clock in the evening of the same day. There will be service in the Church also at 4 o'clock in the afternoon."

Mrs. Furman makes no references to St. Stephen's activities in 1874. However, the new rector evidently soon began to make a decidedly good impression, especially on the writer of a piece in The Union & Recorder for April 8, 1874. It reads in part as follows:

> We were present at the celebration of Easter in St. Stephen's Church last Sunday morning. It has rarely been our fortune to be more impressed with a service than on this festal day of the Church. Joy and gladness seemed to greet us as we entered the Church . . . The church was beautifully dressed with garlands and flowers and appropriate mottoes and the air was redolent with the odor of Spring's floral offerings. Great taste was displayed in the decorations, while there was enough to make it beautiful, there was not that superabundance which sometimes destroys the effect . . . Minister and congregation seemed in unison as evidenced by his impressive rendition of the Church service and the hearty responses of the people.

The editor again paid tribute to the Rev. Mr. Stoney, declaring that "St. Stephen's has reason for congratulations in her Rector, the Rev. Mr. Stoney—recently come among us; be has won the hearts of all. By his quiet but earnest manner he is doing the Master's work well, and with the hearty co-operation of his people the Church will wield that influence upon society in this community for which she was ordained by her Risen Lord." That same issue carried a notice of vestry election on Easter Monday: John S. Thomas and J. W. Herty returned as wardens, as did all the other members: J. W. Wilcox, J. M. Clark, B. R. Herty, F. G. Grieve, F. B. Mapp, T. H. Kenan, F. C. Furman, with F. G. Grieve as secretary and treasurer. J. W. Wilcox was named a delegate to the convention again, as were J. W. Herty and John S. Thomas, with B. R. Herty, J. M. Clark, and W. H. Scott as alternates.

Clearly the rector wasted no time in getting involved in community affairs. A report of a meeting of the Southern Historical Society, printed on April 29, listed the Rev. Mr. Stoney as one of three men named to a committee "to draft a constitution for a permanent organization of an independent Baldwin County Historical Society."

Delegates to the diocesan convention were given treatment more like that reserved for today's CEO's. That same issue carried the news that "Delegates to the Episcopal Convention which meets in Athens on the 6th of May," would be given passes by certain railroads for their transportation.

No explanation was given as to why the Rev. Mr. Lucas returned, but on May 20th, the Union & Recorder ran a short paragraph stating that he would "hold services, preach, and administer the communion in St. Stephen's (Episcopal) Church next Sunday, 24th inst." It concluded with the now customary reminder, "Pews free."

The Rev. Mr. Stoney's activity in community affairs was noted in an account of a Masonic celebration on St. John's Day, July 24, when he "opened and closed the exercises with prayer."

On July 22nd, the paper rejoiced over the success of the latest effort of "the ladies of the Episcopal Church," who "return their most sincere thanks to the citizens of Milledgeville, Midway, and

Scottsboro for their very liberal aid, at their Ice Cream Festival, on the evening of the 16th inst. To Mr. G. T. Wiedenman for the loan of a Piano, Mr. Otto Miller, for Crockery, Messrs. Carakers, for Chairs, and Messrs. W. T. Conn & Co., for use of room." Receipts were reported to be $72.85.

In contrast to some of the lengthy wedding stories, that of "Mr. Wm. P. HUNTER of Savannah, Ga., to Miss MARY J. SMITH, niece of Col. S. N. Boughton of Milledgeville, was confined to six lines on November 11. The service was conducted "On the 5th inst., at St. Stephen's Church, Milledgeville, by the Rev. D. E. Mortimer, Rector of Christ Church, Savannah, assisted by the Rev. Mr. Stoney of St. Stephen's Church."

In addition to raising money for itself, St. Stephen's was involved in community outreach. The Union & Recorder on February 9, 1875, announced a concert to be given that night . . . by the Ladies of the Episcopal Church and others, for the benefit of the Factory Mission School, not only appeals for a liberal patronage on account of the cause, but it promises to be one of the most enjoyable social affairs of the kind offered our citizens this winter. Lovers of good Music, especially, will not fail to attend, as the best talent in the city is (rendered?) for the occasion. By the way we have heard it whispered, that the Hall will be ceased for a dance after the concert.

A short "Funeral Notice" ran on September 14, 1875, for Charles J. duBignon, a member of one of the most prominent Milledgeville families. His friends and family "are invited to attend" the service at "5 o'clock Tuesday, the 14th, from St. Stephen's Church." The grandson of a French Royalist who settled on Jekyll Island, he had "served his country in one of the Indian wars, the Mexican War, and was also a captain in the Confederate War, in Cobbs Legion of Calvary. He was fondly called by his friends, from his gallant and handsome appearance, 'Our French Field Marshal.'" His father-in-law, Seaton Grantland, had established the Milledgeville Recorder. Curiously enough, his obituary was not carried until November 2, when it ran to more than 300 words.

The paper carried a brief announcement on October 12, 1875, of a visit to St. Stephen's by Bishop Beckwith on the 21st: "He will preach in the morning and at night and confirm at night." Finally for 1875, the following appeared in the edition of Tuesday, December 6th:

> The Augusta Convocation, (Episcopal Church) will meet in session to-night 7th, to hold over Wednesday and Thursday. St. Stephen's Church will be open for Divine Service each night of the three days at 7 o'clock, and in the morning of Wednesday and Thursday at 11 o'clock. To which the public is cordially invited.

Below, in a much smaller size type, appeared a complete listing of sermons "upon the four subjects of the Judgment, Heaven, Hell," along with the names of the priests.

How the Rev. Mr. Hugh Roy Scott, of Baltimore, happened to visit St. Stephen's is not explained, but according to a brief notice in the paper on Tuesday, March 21, 1876, "at the regular services, on Friday afternoon," the Rev. Mr. Scott "gave a very interesting account of what the Church is doing in England."

Under the heading "RELIGIOUS," the following appeared on April 11, 1876:

> "There will he Evening Prayer at St. Stephen's every afternoon this week at 5 o'clock, except Saturday—(Passion Week.)
> "Holy Communion Thursday night at 8 o'clock.
> "Morning Prayer Friday morning at 11 o'clock."

The obituary of another communicant, "Miss Lou Crawford, a niece of Capt. C. P. Crawford," appeared in a column of general news briefs on May 9, 1876. "A beautiful and accomplished young lady, " . . . her death has filled the community with sadness. She was buried on Sunday afternoon, with the impressive burial service of the Episcopal Church—her pastor, the Rev. J. M. Stoney officiating."

Bishop Beckwith's "annual visitation to St. Stephen's church of this city, next Sunday, 29th inst.," was noted on October 24. Services would be held at 10:30 am, and 7:30 p.m., the bishop expected to preach at both and administer "the rite of confirmation" in the morning. The bishop, according to the editor on October 31, "preached two fine sermons at the Episcopal Church in this city, last Sabbath." Since another paragraph in the same column gives the number of confirmands as nine, the Rev. Mr. Stoney must have been making some progress in increasing the number of communicants.

St. Stephen's was evidently making progress financially also, for the purchase of "a beautiful lot near the residence of Judge Harris" by St. Stephen's was announced on November 21, 1876. To be used for a parsonage, "the erection of the building will be commenced in a short time."

In the church building itself, weddings continued to be held. Several inches of newsprint are devoted to the wedding on Wednesday (November, 1876) at St. Stephen's of "Mr. William A. Jarratt and Miss Roxie, the only daughter of the late Robt. A. McComb . . . Rev. J. M. Stoney officiating."

After having gone into considerable detail, the editor proclaims, "We venture no description of the happy occasion, but simply say it was characterized by the ease, grace and elegance that might have been expected from Attendants familiar with such scenes."

Marriages brought joy to the parish, which at the same time was subjected to deaths. On December 26, 1876, the Union & Recorder ran a piece several column inches long, headed "DEATH OF DR. JAMES W. HERTY" the junior warden of St. Stephen's and twice mayor of Milledgeville:

> Many of our citizens were not only pained to hear of the
> death of this gentleman, but greatly surprised, for but few
> persons outside of his immediate family and circle of friends

knew that he was ill, until the sad intelligence of his death spread over the city. He died on the morning of the 20th, at his residence.

Some of the events of his life, including his duty first in the United States Navy and then in the Confederate Navy, are recorded. The piece concludes: "Dr. Herty was about 40 years old, and leaves a wife and interesting family, who have our sincere sympathy in their very heavy bereavement." Editors did not hesitate to express their opinions in supposedly straight news stories, but this one did not see fit to explain what he meant by the word "interesting."

A far longer piece, a "Tribute of Respect" from the Benevolent Lodge, No. 3, F.A.M. was reported on January 23, 1877. The committee appointed "to draft suitable resolutions" included the rector of St. Stephen's, the Rev. Mr. Stoney, for his name heads the list. No mention is made in either of those two accounts of Dr. Herty's involvement at St. Stephen's, but a resolution from the church is printed immediately below the Masonic tribute.

A second resolution from the Vestry follows, on a totally different subject: "Resolved, That the Rev. J. M. Stoney be authorized and requested to collect all monies subscribed by the citizens for the building of the Rectory. WM. H. SCOTT, Secretary."

A week later, the paper ran a correction concerning Dr. Herty's age upon being "commissioned Assistant Surgeon in the U. S. Navy." The correction is not very clear, but it does indicate that he had reached the age of 21, for it explains that "on account of his youth" . . . he "was subjected to an unusually rigid examination."

April of that year produced Mrs. Furman's history, which she May 1, 1877. In it, she credits the Rev. Mr. Stoney with "a steady growth" for the parish, "both in number and interest," the number having increased from 34 to 65. She adds, "Despite the pecuniary depression under which the country has laboured, the congregation has recently succeeded in building a comfortable Rectory for the Pastor."

On May 8, 1877, the Rev. Mr. Stoney issued a short notice

that he expected "to be absent next Sunday the 13th inst. There will be, therefore, no services in the Church that day."

During the next week, Dr. Samuel G. White, another "distinguished physician died at his residence." As a result, "in respect to the family and many friends . . . the ladies of the Episcopal Church have postponed their Strawberry & Ice Cream Festival until Tuesday afternoon and evening of May 23, 1877."

On August 2nd, the ladies held a Lawn Party, pronounced in the edition of August 7, 1877, "a pleasant affair, a success socially and financially."

In the next column the ladies expressed their appreciation to their supporters:

> A SUCCESS—The Ladies of the Episcopal Church return their grateful acknowledgements to the citizens of Milledgeville for their very liberal patronage at their Lawn Party on the 2d inst. August 7th, 1877.

Readers were urged on October 30, 1877, to "Go to the concert of the ladies of the Episcopal Church next Friday night and hear some good music and help them in a good cause. We did not attend the last one but hear it was quite enjoyable."

The paper ran a long, detailed new story on December 4, 1877, under the heading "GEORGIA STATISTICS," with the following data but no explanation of the term "sittings": "The Episcopal church has 29 churches, 11,000 sittings, 4,500 communicants, and 39 clergymen."

Occasionally a notice raises more questions than it answers. Readers were told on January 15, 1878, "there were no services at the Episcopal Church last Sabbath, Rev. J. M. Stoney being absent in Sparta."

"THE CHURCHES" column on February 5, 1878, led off with "EPISCOPAL CHURCH—Rev. J. M. Stoney, Rector. Services Sunday at 11 a.m. and 4 p.m. Sabbath school at 10 a.m."

Mrs. Anna Marie Green Cook, who as a young girl had kept a

journal that Professor Bonner edited, wrote a History of Baldwin County Georgia, in which she includes a note on the Rev. Mr. Stoney:

> "The last building remaining" from an "Academy for young ladies was used as a chapel when Rev. J. M. Stoney of St. Stephen's Episcopal Church conducted for many years a flourishing mission church in Scottsboro for the country people living round about."

A parishioner who would later make a significant contribution to St. Stephen's, "the efficient engineer at the Asylum," Capt. John W. Wilcox received recognition on February 19, 1878, for having "organized a fire department, which he will drill until it becomes effective. With a perfect system of water works and a well drilled fire company, no fears of fire needed be apprehended in this institution."

The edition of the Union & Recorder for March 12, 1878, carried the usual notice of services at St. Stephen's as well as an account of the wedding of Dr. H. B. Lee of Atlanta "to Miss Annie Belle, youngest daughter of P. M. Compton, Esq., of this city. The marriage ceremony took place at the Episcopal Church, which was handsomely decorated for the occasion . . . The impressive ceremony of the Episcopal marriage service was read by the Rector, Rev. J. M. Stoney."

St. Stephen's held its annual meeting and election of officers on Easter morning, April 22nd, according to an item in the edition of April 30. J. S. Thomas Sr. was retained as senior warden and J. W. Wilcox, Jr., named junior warden. Vestrymen B. R. Herty, F. C. Furman, Frank B. Mapp, and Fleming G. Grieve were returned, along with newcomers Howard Tinsley, O. H. Fox, W. W. Williamson, and W. H. Scott. "At a subsequent meeting of the vestry, Messrs. B. R. Herty, W. H. Scott, and J. W. Wilcox were chosen delegates to the convention to assemble in Augusta on the 15th of May . . . Rector J. M. Stoney presided at these meetings with Mr. W. H. Scott as secretary."

Maintaining the church required repairs, to be financed at least in part by a festival, reported on May 7 as having taken place "last Thursday evening," when enough money was raised" to make some of them. A month later, on June 11, the repairs were reported as "being made." Despite the financial needs of St. Stephen's, the church did not hesitate to contribute to a yellow-fever fund, according to a story in the edition of September 24:

> St. Stephens Church, Rev. J. M. Stoney, Rector, sent by Express on Saturday last to the St. Mary's (Episcopal) Sisterhood at Memphis, one hundred dollars, to be used in aid of the yellow fever sufferers in that city. This collection was made among the members of St. Stephen's Church.

"The Episcopal Church, the Rev. Mr. Stoney, Rector," is the first listed under the heading THE CHURCHES in The Union & Recorder on August 13, 1878. Services were being held at 11. a.m., and 7 p.m., on Sunday, with "Sabbath school at 10 a.m."

Another vestryman and Civil War veteran, Capt. B. R. Herty, died on October 7, 1878, according to the Union & Recorder on October 8. The next week's edition noted in a column of miscellaneous items that "The death of Capt. Herty and Mr. Otto Miller is a severe loss to our community. Elsewhere the paper ran a long obituary under the heading "OBSEQUIES OF CAPT. B. R. HERTY," beginning with an apology for the previous short notice. The entire service is detailed; it must have involved the most pomp and ceremony of any event since before the war:

> The pageant was sadly imposing, and to the slow and solemn notes of the Dead March the procession moved to St. Stephen's (Episcopal) church, of which Capt. Herty was a member . . . The services here were conducted very appropriately by the rector, Rev. J. M. Stoney. Then at the grave, the Rev. Mr. Stoney read the beautiful burial service.

The same issue carried the obituary for Mr. Otto Miller, a recent but unsuccessful candidate for mayor of Milledgeville:

> Those who read our brief notice last week of the critical
> condition of Mr. Miller will not be surprised to read the
> announcement of his death, which took place at his residence
> in this city, at half past one o'clock Wednesday morning last,
> of an affection of the lungs, complicated with heart disease
> [after having] been confined to his bed about one month.

His exact age the day of his death was given: 28 years and one month. A native of Milledgeville, he was married to Miss Laura Bethune, also of Milledgeville, who, with two children, survived him. "The funeral services were held at the family residence, and conducted by Rev. J. M. Stoney," the first mention of any connection with St. Stephen's. At the grave, the rector also read "the impressive burial service of the Protestant Episcopal Church."

The editor observes, "The death of two such men as Mr. Miller, and Capt. Herty, within a few days of each other—both young— both living on the same street—each having but two children— and buried by the same officiating clergyman, are coincidences striking in themselves."

The Vestry did not get around to a resolution as "an expression of our personal regard for" Capt. Herty, "and our high estimate of his value" until December, with the notice appearing on December 2nd.

The bishop's visit was noted on December. 3, 1878: "Bishop Beckwith will preach at St. Stephen's Church, in this city, next Sunday morning and night. The morning service will include the confirmation of a class." As usual, the bishop made a most favorable impression on the editor, who reported on December 10 reported that he "had not the pleasure of hearing Bishop Beckwith's sermon on Sabbath morning, but it was our privilege to be one of a large and intelligent audience on Sunday night." His sermon was described as "a masterly eloquent and impressive exposition of the ways of God and the duty of Man."

The editor adds that "It would be presumptuous in us to attempt to analyze either the soundness or the sentiments of the sermon," though he did feel "the charm—we gave ourselves up to it, but we strive in vain to analyze it." He again comments that when the bishop chose the pulpit, "the stage lost a king of the first magnitude. With his faultless physique, splendid voice and graceful oratory, he would have adorned the highest realms of tragedy," The account also reported that the bishop confirmed three persons, "two white and one colored."

The rector's preaching in the Swainsboro Baptist church warranted a notice in the Swainsboro Herald that was copied by the Union & Recorder on January 21, 1879. He "delighted his hearers."

The ladies never stopped their fund-raising activities. The next week's edition informed readers of a "supper for the benefit of the Church, on Friday night, January 31st." The affair reportedly brought in $70.

The results of the election of officers at St. Stephen's on Easter Monday, April 14, 1879, were announced on April 29:

> William W. Williamson, F. C. Furman, F. B. Mapp, F. G. Grieve, and W. H. Scott were returned with Jas. Lees and T. H. Kenan replacing Howard Tinsley and the late B. R. Herty. Both Mr. Scott and Mr. Wilcox were named again as delegates to the convention that meets in Marietta second Monday in May, along with Mr. Lees. Mr. Scott was listed as treasurer as well as secretary.

Obviously, the Rev. Mr. Stoney kept up with activities in Milledgeville, and his opinions were respected. He felt compelled to write the following letter on June 30, 1879, regarding a recent spelling bee in which apparently a team of boys opposed one of girls. The letter, dated June 30th, 1879, appeared on July 1 and reads in part:

> I think that the proficiency in many regards of the scholars of Mr. Cone's school, as it was manifested in the examination

of last week, deserves the expressed commendation of some
who were present . . . I desire to call attention especially to
the school's training in spelling.

An account of Bishop Beckwith's visit "last Sabbath" when he
"confirmed a class of seven," appeared on November 11, 1879.
His "sermon on that occasion was intensely interesting . . . At night
the bishop preached a magnificent sermon, proving the truth of
the Christian religion by its triumphant progress in the world,
against all the obstacles of human prejudice and imperial power
and pagan persecution." The last paragraph of the item seemingly
contradicts the first statement, for it gives as "fourteen persons in
all" whom the bishop confirmed "during his visit to the city."

In the same issue, the editor acknowledges that he had "had a
call on Wednesday from Rev. Joshua Knowles of Greensboro. He
was in attendance upon the Convocation of the Episcopal Clergy,
in this city. The happiness of greeting him was a pleasure we missed
at home, by being absent at the Fair." What happened? Did the
editor go to the fair and miss the bishop?

The adjacent column carries the following, under the heading
AUGUSTA CONVOCATION:

> The clergy of the Episcopal Church occupying parishes
> within the Missionary district of Augusta Convocation, came
> together at St. Stephen's Church last week, to transact the
> usual routine of business of the Convocation.

Their names were then given, including that of the dean, the Rev.
C. C. Williams, who "preached in the chapel of asylum . . . The
next meeting of the Convocation was appointed to be held in
Madison on the fourth Tuesday in April, 1880."

On March 23, 1880, appeared the obituary of "little ARCHIE,
son of Mr. James A. Jarratt, Jr., on Monday, March 15th, 1880.
Aged two years and eight, he was lamented in several lines of verse.

The toddler died after "a short illness of a few hours, from
congestion of the lungs . . . He had been baptized about a year

ago, in the Episcopal Church, and the burial service of the Church was read over his little body early in the morning of Tuesday, by the Rev. Mr. Stoney."

It was time for another Vestry election, reported on April 6 as having been held on Easter Monday. John S. Thomas and J. W. Wilcox were returned as wardens; W. W. Williamson, F. C. Furman, also named secretary and treasurer, F. B. Mapp, F. G. Grieve, Dr. T. H. Kenan, and W. H. Scott as members of the Vestry, with Dr. T. H. Kenan replacing O. H. Fox.

J. W. Wilcox and W. H. Scott were again named "Delegates to the Diocesan Convention, to meet at Trinity Church, Columbus, Ga., on Wednesday, May 19th, 1880." Vestryman Williamson replaced B. R. Herty as a delegate. W. H. Scott continued as secretary.

Clearly, the rector's activities as well as those of St. Stephen's merited attention in the December 14 issue of the Union & Recorder, which copied from an Augusta paper a report that he said Evening Prayer at the Augusta Convocation at St. Paul's Church "last night . . . The Rev. Mr. Stoney will preach at night at 8 o'clock."

✟ ✟ ✟

Then & Now: The interweaving of parish and community life has been an ongoing issue in the life of St. Stephen's. It is interesting to see how much attention was given in the newspaper accounts to the community activities of the Rev. Mr. Stoney. Years later, the Rev. F. Harriman Harding—St. Stephen's longest-standing rector of the twentieth century—continued the tradition was listed in the July 3, 1950, edition of the Atlanta Journal-Constitution *as "a leader in cultural, humanitarian and civic endeavors." Also like Stoney, Harding's accomplishments and influence extended beyond the parish. The son and grandson of clergymen, Harding's "record of service" includes being . . .*

for nearly a quarter of century secretary of the diocese of Atlanta, . . . a member and secretary of the standing committee of the dioceses and of the board of officers of the

corporation, . . . chairman of the committee on constitution
and canons, . . . former executive secretary and treasurer of
the missionary funds, editor of the Diocesan Record and a
member of the executive board [and two-time elected
deputy] of the triennial convention of the national church.

*The Atlanta article, written by Florence Moran to commemorate the
fiftieth anniversary of Mr. Harding's ordination, notes that the rector
came to St. Stephen's in 1924 after previously having served a parish in
Camden, South Carolina for twelve years. The columnist noted the
Milledgeville rector's intriguing connections: "The minister is a
contemporary and life-long friend of the Hollywood producer, Cecile B.
de Mille." There is little doubt that the Rev. Mr. Harding was indeed
an impressive figure. A anecdotal story has been related regarding a
potential race riot one night in Milledgeville, in the latter part of Mr.
Harding's tenure. It is said that, upon receiving a call about the rising
tensions, the rector immediately got to the scene of danger and somehow
calmed down the factions, thereby single-handedly resolving the situation.
Whether this incident is entirely factual, the story certainly shows the
high esteem in which Mr. Harding was held. Few rectors have been as
active and respected in so many arenas as this faithful worker.*

*It is particularly interesting to note in the account of the Rev. Mr.
Stoney's rectorship the creation of "an independent Baldwin County
Historical Society." As a vital historical landmark itself, St. Stephen's
has often been the subject of discussion and interest by that society. Although
at times there have been struggles between parish and society, the most
well-known of which involved a dispute over the preservation or removal
of a historic tree on church property, more often than not, there has been
mutual appreciation of the work both parties do in safeguarding the heritage
that we in Milledgeville have inherited. Parishioners such as Mary Jones,
Jan Hardy, and others have been active members of the Historical Society
and, in Hardy's case, carried out extensive research in Milledgeville's
newspaper accounts, vestry minutes, and other records. Indeed, readers not
only of this book, but also of a series of writings on the history of First
Methodist Church, are indebted to her conscientious research.*

5

Tough Times: The 1880s

St. Stephen's suffered a stunning loss in January, 1881, when Colonel John Sherrod Thomas died. He had served as senior warden from 1859 until his death on January 9. Despite the shorter life expectancy in the nineteenth century, he—and his parents—defied the odds. His lengthy obituary appeared on January 18, 1881, and identified him as a veteran of the War of 1812, marshal of the day when Lafayette visited Milledgeville, a former state representative, and judge of the Inferior Court and included a good deal of the history of the area but failed to mention his connection to St. Stephen's:

> Col. J. S. Thomas was . . . the son of Martha Walker and
> James Thomas . . . Martha Thomas died in Midway in 1856,
> at the age of 100 years. James, her husband, died in Hancock,
> at the age of 97.

A single sentence assures notice in this twenty-first century account of St. Stephen's: "In 1866 he became a member of the Protestant Episcopal church." The obituary then comes to a comparatively short conclusion:

> The funeral of the late Judge John S. Thomas took place
> on Tuesday from the Episcopal Church in this city. The
> Rev. J. M. Stoney, the pastor, conducted the impressive
> services. The remains were followed to the cemetery by a

large number of citizens, notwithstanding the extreme inclemency of the day.

Few public servants of today would receive such attention. Readers are reminded on Jan. 25, 1881, that Lent begins in "only about six weeks . . . The weather has sadly marred festivities since the beginning of the Christmas holidays. The gay world, who put on the somber garb during the Lenten season, will have but a few weeks now in which to shoot folly as it flies, and sip from the ambrosial cup of pleasure." The editor must have been rather well-read in English literature, for he took the phrase "shoot folly as it flies" from Alexander Pope's Essay on Man.

The subject of temperance received much attention in the last half of the nineteenth century. Two paragraphs below the obituary inform readers that "The Rev. J. M. Stoney, by appointment, will preach next Sunday morning, the 30th inst., in St. Stephen's Church, upon the subject of 'drunkenness and the prohibition law,' and will enforce his arguments by relating the consequences of drunkenness as observed in the inside of an Insane Asylum."

Vestry resolutions, then as now, require time. The one from a committee at St. Stephen's on February 1, 1881, should have left no doubt in the minds of Union-Recorder readers of the esteem with which Col. Thomas was held by St. Stephen's. It reads in part as follows:

> The Rector and congregation of St. Stephen's Church would hereby place on record an expression of their respect and affection for their friend and Senior Warden J. S. Thomas, deceased, January 10th, A. D. 1880 (sic).
>
> One of the oldest and most esteemed citizens of Milledgeville, he was recognized as a gentlemen and a faithful son of his State. Since the organization of the parish, he has been in some prominent way connected with its history, having almost constantly represented the parish in the Diocesan Councils, until the weight of his years compelled

him to withdraw from active labors. He filled the office of
Senior Warden from 1859, to the date of his death.

He loved the Church; was loyal to its interests; and was
active in promoting its advancement and welfare, and the
parish feels it a privilege to be able to offer this tribute of
respect to his memory.

We hereby convey to the bereaved family of our friend,
an expression of profound sympathy, and humbly trust
that they may receive comfort and consolation from the
great Source of all comfort.

It was signed by the Rev. J. M. Stoney, W. H. Scott, and F. G.
Grieve.

At that time, the pastor of the Methodist Episcopal Church,
as it was called then, was apparently rather new to his congregation,
because the obituary on February 1, 1881, for Mrs. Elizabeth R.
Fair notes that he was "not intimately acquainted with her." His
comments at her funeral were followed by "appropriate remarks"
by "Rev. Mr. Stoney, of the Episcopal Church."

"Bishop Beckwith," according to the Union-Recorder on
February 8, "was in Albany Sunday, 30th, and delivered his address
on temperance." He also had "made the appointment for his annual
visit to St. Stephen's Church, for Sunday, February 27th, 1881."

On February 22nd, the paper again reported on the bishop:
"Bishop Beckwith will preach in St. Stephen's Church, God willing,
at the morning service 11:00 and evening service seven and half
o'clock." The letter made no reference to God and reporting on
the first day of March Bishop Beckwith "preached two able
discourses on Sunday last at St. Stephen's Church to large
congregations. Five persons received the rite of confirmation."

On April 12, 1881 10 Union & Recorder ran the obituary for
Mr. E. J. White whose funeral was conducted at the family residence
by the Rev. J. M. Stoney. No church affiliation was given. The
same issue of the paper contains a petition signed by J. M. Stoney
and three others asking the trustees of the recently established
middle Georgia Military and Agricultural College to except for its

library "books from Oglethorpe University." Below the petition
appears the acceptance by the trustees with the regulations for the
use of the books. No explanation is given regarding how the books
came into the care of the rector and the committee on which he
served. But again the no-shows the involvement of the rector in
community affairs. The college had been established two years
earlier on state health square. It is now known as Georgia Military
College and is still located on land immediately behind the St.
Stephen's.

On May 3rd the paper reported that "the Rev. J. M. Stoney
will leave today to attend the Episcopal convention which assembles
in Savannah." The same issue also carried results of the vestry
election on April 13th when several changes were made. W. H.
Scott became senior warden with J. W. Wilcox continuing as junior
warden. W. W. Williamson, Dr. T. H. Kenan, and F. Brandt were
returned to the vestry with the addition of F. B. Henderson succeeding
F. B. Mapp. F. G. Grieve became secretary and treasurer in place of F.
C. Furman. Delegates to the convention included two new ones F. B.
Henderson and H. Turner as well as W. H. Scott.

Picnics (spelled as two words, "pic nics"), seemed very popular
in Milledgeville at that time. The paper for May 17th reported
that "the Sunday School of the Protestant Episcopal Church in
this city will pic nic on Saturday next May 21st at old Fort
Wilkinson. It is a beautiful spot about to 2 mi. from the city. If the
day is pleasant we doubt not that all that participate will have a
splendid time."

Interest in temperance apparently ran high in Milledgeville,
for on May 24th the paper carried a notice from the Midway
Community that . . .

> The Midday Society for the Promotion of Temperance is
> steadily increasing in numbers. Rev. J. M. Stoney is president.
> General B. M. Thomas is secretary. One of St. Stephen's
> vestrymen, Dr. T. H. Kenan, has been invited to deliver an
> address before the Midway Society on the third Tuesday
> night in June. He has accepted and any in the public

interested are cordially invited to be present. Further notice will be given.

In August at St. Stephen's lost another of its communicants, Mrs. M. J. Kenan whose obituary appeared on August 30th:

> Married to Capt. M. J. Kenan, and resided in this city nearly her entire married life. She leaves for children, two sons, and two daughters, all married, Viz: Dr. Spalding Kenan, of McIntosh County, Mrs. Dr. C. H. Hall, of Macon, Mrs. W. W. Williamson, of Milledgeville, and Capt. O. T. Kenan of the same city. She died at the residence of her daughter in Macon. The remains reached Milledgeville on Tuesday and were taken to the Episcopal Church of which she had long been a communicant, where services were held by the rector, Rev. J. M. Stoney.

Both daughters were identified by their husbands' names according to the custom of the day. One was married to a vestryman, W. W. Williamson. Notice that the other was identified by her husband's title, "Mrs. Dr. C.H. Hall," a common practice in some parts until the middle of the twentieth century.

The ladies never quit, as on September 6th the paper ran a notice under "THE CITY" that those of the "Sunday School will have a festival next Thursday, September 8th, at the store next door to Mr. J. M. Clark's drugstore commencing at 5:00 in the afternoon and continuing after dark. They will be pleased to see all and serve them with nice refreshments." Another obituary appeared in the Union & Recorder on September 20, 1881, that of Mrs. O. H. Fox who died "at her father's residence in Augusta on Wednesday morning . . . She was a member of the Protestant Episcopal Church of the city." The account concludes with details of the service held at the Episcopal Church at 5:00 p.m. Thursday and . . . conducted by the pastor Rev. J. M. Stoney."

Meanwhile, on the national scene, James Abram Garfield, senator from Ohio and formal Union Army general, had been

elected president in 1880 to succeed President Grant. Inaugurated
on March 4, 1881, he served only five months before being shot
on July 2nd in a Washington Railway Station in route to Williams
College in Williamstown, Massachusetts. He lingered until
September 19th when the vice-president, Chester A. Arthur, took
office (Morris, 256). On September 27th, the Union and Recorder
ran the following notice:

> In accordance with the proclamation of President Arthur
> and his honor Mayor Walker, memorial services were held at
> St. Stephen's Church by the pastor Rev. J. M. Stoney and at
> the Methodist Church at 11:00. We attended the latter.

On October 18th, the Rev. Mr. Stoney's re-election as chaplain of
the asylum was duly noted under the personal columns and on
November 8th a notice was reprinted from a source identified only
by abbreviations: "The Rev. J. M. Stoney of Milledgeville . . . has
kindly offered to officiate and administer the Holy Communion at
Christ Church next Sunday morning." Readers were also notified
in that edition that "Bishop Beckwith will be in this city on Sunday
the 27th inst., and hold services in St. Stephen's Church in the
morning sermon and confirmation. At night he will deliver by
request a lecture on Temperance."

A final notice for St. Stephen's in 1881 appeared on November
29th under the heading "Bishop Beckwith" who "preached a most
impressive sermon at St. Stephen's Church in the city last Sunday
morning and confirmed a class of nine persons among whom was
Dr. T. H. Kenan, First Assistant Physician of the State Lunatic
Asylum." Curiously enough, in May the physician had been elected
to the vestry, a position that now requires members to have been
confirmed. The newspaper account continues: "At night the church
was filled to overflowing to hear the bishops great sermon on
Temperance," which was then summarized at considerable length.

The year 1882 began with another loss for St. Stephen's, and
certainly a difficult one for the widow whose mother had died the
previous August. The Union & Recorder printed a lengthy obituary

on January 10th: "We are deeply pained to record the death of Captain William W. Williamson, which occurred at his residence in this city on Wednesday morning last" from" dreadful disease consumption." The funeral of the vestryman and former member of the Georgia Legislature "took place from his residence Friday at 11:00 a.m., Rev. J. M. Stoney, rector of St. Stephen's Church, officiating. The pallbearers were Messrs. D.B. Sanford, E.C. Furman, F.G. duBignon, R. Whitfield, A. Joseph, Dr. I.L. Harris, F.B. Mapp, and P.M. Compton." A week later, the edition of January 17th carried a notice concerning another communicant, though she was not identified as such:

> We are pained to hear of the severe illness of Miss Lucy Tinsley. For some time she has spent a great sufferer from rheumatism; but last week condition was much more unfavorable and caused her many personal friends sorrow and apprehension.

Unfortunately the editor's concern was justified, for the next week's issue, for January 24th, carried her obituary. Once more, "the funeral services were held at the family residence at 3:00 Tuesday afternoon and were conducted by Rev. J. M. Stoney, rector of St. Stephen's Church, of which the deceased was a communicant." Two weeks after the obituary for Capt. Williamson, a tribute of respect appeared in the Union & Recorder, one part of which notes that "in honor of his memory, and in token of our grief at his deceased, we will cause a blank leaf to be left in our book of minutes, with his name inscribed there."

On February 28th, the paper noted the beginning of Lent:

> Wednesday last was Ash Wednesday, the beginning of the season of Lent. It is a season of 40 days of great solemnity with the Protestant Episcopal and Catholic churches, the former fasting on Wednesday and Saturday of each week as well as on the Ember days and Holy Thursday. Early Mass is secretly observed by the faithful of the latter Church.

Observance of Easter service was reported on April 11th:

> Easter Sunday—St. Stephen's Church was beautifully
> decorated with the rarest and prettiest flowers that could be
> obtained. Rev. J. M. Stoney preached an eloquent and artists
> sermon, which was followed by the Lord's Supper, to which
> all Christians present were invited. The attendance was
> unusually large.

Even in the 1880s, apparently, communicants realized the necessity of attending the Easter service.

On April 18th, the Union & Recorder duly noted the vestry election at St. Stephen's. William H. Scott, Sr. was returned as senior warden and J. W. Wilcox Jr. as junior warden. Hatch Turner replaced the late Capt. Williamson. Dr. Thomas H. Kenan, F. C. Furman, and F. G. Grieve were reelected, the latter also as secretary. William H. Scott was again named as a delegate to the "convention to meet in Madison in May." He was joined by newcomers Dr. Kenan and Mr. Wilcox.

On May 2nd was reported the "ice cream and strawberry Festival, next Friday evening, May 5th, in the Hall of their Royal Arcanum . . . from 6 o'clock to 10 o'clock. The patronage of the public is respectfully solicited." St. Stephen's lost another communicant later that month, the widow of the late Col. J. S. Thomas; her obituary appeared on June 6th:

> There fell asleep in Jesus, and the communion of the church
> and in the hope of a joyful resurrection, May 15th, 1882,
> MRS. ELIZA HESTER THOMAS, aged 82 years, eight
> months in three days, at the residence of her son, Mr. Henry
> Thomas in Midway.

Obviously, St. Stephen's Church made its presence felt in the community: "As a communicant of the Episcopal Church, she is identified with the beginning and growth of St. Stephen's Parish, and by her devotion to her church, she was a living example of what can be performed by one whose heart is filled with love to God and man." Interestingly enough, the rector's initials followed the piece.

Not only did the rector get around but the local paper kept up with his itinerary. The Union & Recorder must have kept up an extensive exchange, for the following appeared on July 4, 1882: "We see from the Kingston N.Y. papers that the Rev. James M. Stoney preached twice in that city to large and attentive congregations." He obviously was still taking an active part in civic events. Readers were advised on October 3rd: "At the regular meeting of the young men's prayer meeting next Monday night Rev. Mr. Stoney will deliver a lecture on the subject of Christian unity. All males invited to attend."

The fact that St. Stephen's would host the forthcoming Augusta Convocation meeting was announced in the edition of October 24th, the sessions to begin "this (Tuesday) evening" and continue for "two or three days." A follow-up paragraph appeared the following week October 31st:

> On Thursday we had the pleasure of meeting Rev. Joshua Knowles of Greensboro, who was attending the Episcopal Convention. The writer has known Mr. Knowles ever since he knew anybody, and in all the changes and through all the troubles of the times, since our first acquaintance, we have ever found him the same polished, courteous, Christian gentleman. Mr. Knowles, in addition to his ministerial duties, conducts with his son when of the purest and best papers in the state, "The Home Journal."

The following week, the Union & Recorder copied a long piece from the aforementioned *Home Journal* on the visit to Milledgeville by the Home Journal owner. Parts of it follow:

> The attendance upon the convocation was not as large as usual, but the services were quite interesting and we trust profitable. The weather could not have been more

delightful. Many sad changes have taken place in Milledgeville since we resided there, and where we passed some of the happiest years of our life. Few of the old inhabitants remain . . . The Baptist, Methodist and Presbyterian churches have recently been improved and, we were glad to learn, are supplied with able and devoted pastors. The Rev. Mr. Stoney, the worthy rector of the Episcopal Church, in addition to his parochial labors, officiates regularly at the insane asylum.

Because of the "many improvements . . . made at the old capital since its location there," the article concluded that "Milledgeville and vicinity lost nothing by the removal of the seat of government to Atlanta, but the State has evidently lost by the change."

Bishop Beckwith's annual visitation was noted on November 28th: "Bishop Beckwith of the Episcopal Diocese of Georgia preached at St. Stephen's Church in the city on Sunday last, and confirmed a class of five. The bishop is a learned and eloquent Divine." A paragraph on December 19th shows that pre-Christmas shopping is not a new incident:

Next Saturday will be made to serve for Christmas Eve. Sunday, bearing the honors this year, will be very generally observed in the Catholic and Episcopal churches. Saturday will be the jolly trading day. And we fear many will not be in a churchgoing mood on the Sunday following.

On February 20, 1883, the Union & Recorder printed "LENTEN PASTORAL," a 200-word piece written by the Rev. Mr. Stoney. The results of the election of officers "by the parish of St. Stephen's" on Easter Monday, March 27th were reported on April 3rd. Both the senior and junior wardens, William H. Scott and John W. Wilcox Jr., respectively, were returned to their posts. Thomas H. Kenan, Farish C. Furman, and Fleming G. Grieve the return to the vestry, and E. G. Booth was added, F. G. Grieve being named elected secretary and treasurer. Dr. Kenan and John W. Wilcox were named "delegates to the next convention, to assemble at Albany, the second of May next." Hatch Turner was the third deligate, replacing. William H. Scott.

In April of 1883 were taken the first steps towards St. Stephen's "most dramatic reconstruction and renovation," which left "in the same style and form that which remains almost a century later." That same issue of the Union & Recorder carried the following:

> The congregation of St. Stephen's Episcopal Church being desirous of remodeling and enlarging their place of worship, proposed giving on next Friday evening the 6th inst, for the purpose of raising, in part, the funds for so doing. The programme will be varied and attractive . . . Admission 25¢. Children 15¢, or two tickets for [illegible]. Colored people 15¢ and 10¢. Private boxes seating four persons two dollars (Bonner, St. S).

The following note of appreciation appeared the following week:

> The pastor and congregation of St. Stephen's Church returned their grateful acknowledgments to the public who so liberally patronize their late entertainment; into the ladies and gentlemen outside of the congregation, who so ably contributed to its success.

A separate notice also appeared in that issue: "The concert, or entertainment, at Brake's Opera House last Friday evening was a decided success, financially and otherwise. The audience was large and composed of our best people. The amount realized in behalf of St. Stephen's Episcopal Church, was $62,40 (sic)."

A very personal and poignant notice appeared on May 8th: "Rev. and Mrs. J. M. Stoney lost an infant on Friday. It was buried on Saturday—Reverend Mr. Williams, of Augusta, officiating."

Later that month, on May 25th, the laity went back into action to help finance the remodeling by giving "an ice cream festival." the success of the affair was noted the following week: "The ice cream festival given by the ladies of St. Stephen's Church Friday evening realized over $80 and they return their thanks to the ladies and gentlemen who aided them by their contributions and otherwise." In the next column appeared a news story about the project. Apparently it had prompted an "impromptu meeting of the congregation . . . at the morning services last Sunday" to consider "the question of repairing and remodeling the church building."

> From a rough estimate submitted by Capt. Wilcox, it was ascertained that $1,800 would be required. Those who were present subscribed $355 and determined that the work should be begun at once, and requested the rector to call upon each member of the parish to subscribe to this project (sic).
>
> On motion, but the following persons were appointed as a building committee, VIZ F. C. Furman, O. Fox, Jos. Staley, Adolph Joseph, John W. Wilcox. Rev. James M. Stoney was elected treasurer of the fund.
>
> Member of the congregation was urgently requested to use every effort to raise the required amount. The meeting adjourned.

The edition of June 26, 1883, confirmed in two lines that the Rev. Mr. Stoney was still performing weddings: "Married by the Rev. J. M. Stoney, Mr. G. W. Wright to Mrs. A.C. Bryant, June 5th." The next column carried the program for commencement exercises July 1-July 4 at Middle Georgia Military and Agricultural College, where the "commencement sermon will be preached in the college chapel by Rev. C. C. Williams of Augusta. Services begin at 11:00 a.m." Another item noted that he would "also preach in St. Stephen's, on the 9th, at 8:00."

The local paper continued to keep up with the activities of the bishop. It printed and extensive interview with them by reporter in Chicago, though the headline is somewhat misleading:

> BISHOP BECKWITH ON THE NEGRO AND
> LIQUOR PROBLEMS.
> Chicago, July 10th—the Right Rev. J W Beckwith (,)
> the Episcopal bishop of Georgia, preached here Sunday.
> After the sermon a reporter had a talk with him in regard to
> the progress of the Negro's in the South in the religious and
> general way.

The reporter quoted the Bishop verbatim without any paraphrasing. The bishop blamed the "Negro problems" primarily on the rice plantations, but went on to declare that "liquor is the great curse of civilization everywhere." He offered a solution then that is being put forward today to help curb smoking:

> I believe in controlling it by a system of high taxation. It is
> the best plan in the world to control the traffic. I have
> studied the question for years and I am convinced that you
> cannot stop men from drinking liquor who want to drink it
> by prohibitory legislation. This has been proved.

Despite what the bishop knew and predicted, more than thirty years later the government did try to stop alcohol consumption through legislation with National Prohibition. As the bishop prophesied, Prohibition failed in its purpose, lasting only from 1919 to 1933. Turning his attention again to his primary concern, the bishop maintained:

> We are doing vast good among the Negroes through the
> churches in the South. The Methodists have a large institution
> in Georgia for educating colored preachers, and we have a
> similar one in North Carolina. At the next general convention,
> to be held in October, something will be done in this direction.

The last of this month there will be a conference of Southern Episcopal bishops at Sewanee University in Tennessee to consider the best methods to further the church among the Negroes. I have in my Diocese three or more Negro church schools, to missions, and one parish; but my theory is that there is not so much to be done through the parishes as in the schools. There we can get to the young and educate them and get them divorced from the superstitions of the plantations.

St. Stephen's must have been devastated at the news in the Union & Recorder on September 18, 1883. On that date appeared an obituary for another prominent citizen, a true Renaissance man, the husband of a communicant who wrote probably the first (albeit brief) history of St. Stephen's, a vestryman (despite the fact that he apparently had never been baptized, much less confirmed), a descendant of the man for whom a prominent South Carolina University was named, and a politician who tried to move the capital back to Milledgeville. The headline reads, "DEATH OF HON. F. C. FURMAN," with the long first paragraph consisting of a fulsome tribute. There follows a lengthy biography in which he is consistently referred to as "Judge" although nowhere among the many details of his life does one appear to explain why he was so called: "Too young to be an active participant in the first years of the war . . . his dauntless spirit and brave young heart carried him, young as he was, into the strife, and the last year of the war he was a gallant private in Elliott's South Carolina brigade." Details of his career were then given:

> Always a Democrat. He was elected senator for the 20th District in 1876 for four years but this senatorial term was cut short by the calling of a constitutional convention-a measure he supported with all the ardor of his nature, hoping that the convention restore the capital to Milledgeville.

He was elected to the Constitutional Convention in 1877, and made a useful member. During the capital campaign which followed—the location of the capital as having been left to a vote of the people—he took an active part, making speeches in many counties in favor of returning the seat of government to the "halls of our fathers."

The editor called him "a good speaker, but not always a discreet (sic) politician." In addition to all his connections in politics, he also made a name for himself in the agricultural world:

For the past five or six years, while continuing the practice of law, he devoted most of this time to farming . . . he took 60 a. of land that produced eight bales of cotton the first year he cultivated it, and by intensive farming in the application of the compost that he called a perfect cotton food, he raised the yield steadily until it reached 80 bales from 60 acres. He expected to make from the same ground this year 100 bales, and much interest has been manifested in his growing crop. He published to the world his formula, for the benefit of farmers, . . . the publication of his speeches on his system had made him one of the best known men in the State . . . .

[Furman] became homesick with malarial fever . . . on Friday morning and he grew worse rapidly, and it was known that his illness was unto death. He was baptized by Rev. J. M. Stoney, rector of St. Stephen's Episcopal Church in this city, and received the communion. We learned that he expressed himself as willing and ready to die. At eight and one-half o'clock p.m. Friday, he breathed his last. His funeral took place from the Episcopal Church at 5:00 p.m. Saturday, Rev. J. M. Stoney officiating, and was largely attended. The pallbearers were Messrs. Miller Grieve, E. C. Ramsey, T. W. Turk, John. G. Thomas, C. W. Ennis, Walter Paine, Geo. D. Case and J. W. Wilcox.

The editors simply did not want to let Judge Furman go. The obituary concludes with more detailed financial information than is given today:

> Judge Furman was a member of the Royal Arcanum and the American Legion of Honor, membership in the former society carrying a life insurance of $3,000 and the latter, $5,000. We are glad to note this thoughtfulness on the part of a devoted husband and father. While he possessed fine business sense and made money with the ease, he spent it with a liberal hand. His life insurance enables his family to an unencumbered estate.

Although poetry almost never graces the pages of any newspaper today, verses were frequently printed in all newspapers of the nineteenth century. It is no surprise to find an unsigned one about him at the top of the column next to the obituary.

Immediately below it appear the comments from the Atlanta Journal, a under the heading, "DEATH OF HON. F. C. FURMAN." Clearly his efforts in agriculture were recognized beyond Baldwin County, for the Atlanta paper also commented on them:

> The death of this promising young man is peculiarly felt by people whose eyes had so suddenly been turned upon him by his successful farming enterprises, and his probable solution of the problem that is puzzling our people. The remarkable feature in his life was the abandonment of a lucrative law practice and the most promising field of political preferment to devote his talent and energy to the practical demonstration George's resources in the agricultural line. His name was already familiar all over the South, and he was doing much to encourage the tillers of the soil, and bring that noble calling to a proper estimation in the minds of Southern people.

The Atlanta paper, which did not refer to him as "judge," called his death "a public calamity, and will be mourned all over the State."

The same issue of the Milledgeville paper that carried the Furman obituary devoted much of its space to a story on Bishop Beckwith, whom the editor held in the highest esteem. The bishop had preached at St. Philip's, Atlanta, a sermon that he had given in Chicago, one that violated almost beyond measure today's dictate that one never exceed twenty minutes in length. The sermon's general subject was science versus religion, and the editor described it as "splendid." Noted as the "foremost orator in the South," Bishop Beckwith is further praised by the unidentified author of the piece: "I do not believe that he has a superior in the North." Today's reader should not presume that the Bishop's talents were restricted to the pulpit: "In addition to these qualities of the orator, Bishop Beckwith has a powerful and original mind and strikes out new and impressive lines of thought and rich veins of intellectual inquiry." Clearly, the bishop had impressed the editor, who proclaimed, "I cannot give you the sermon in its entirety, would do it injustice, and yet I cannot refrain from presenting a skeleton of it." The writer comments about his efforts at summarization:

> Reading over my summary of this grand sermon I feel inadequate in my attempt to portray it. It must be given in its entirely, with all of its links of logic and color of illustration, and with the orator's imperial eloquence, to put it with proper effect. No cold and imperfect synopsis can do justice. And yet it deserves aforementioned as an earnest and potential remonstrance and arguments against the growing infidelity of the times.

Most twenty-first-century readers would agree that the sermon was given "warm mention." The piece is signed, "RICHMOND," an indication that, despite the fact that the newspaper is listed simply as *The Chronicle*, likely an Augusta paper, inasmuch as Augusta is in Richmond County.

St. Stephen's rector seemed frequently to be present in the midst of tragic times. The Union & Recorder told its readers on October 9, 1883, of the death of one of the co-owners of the paper, William Barnes. A native of Massachusetts, he had "come to Milledgeville over 40 years ago and took position in the federal union office . . . At his death, Mr. Barnes and Mr. J. N. Moore were sole proprietors of the Union & Recorder." The Rev. Mr. Stoney conducted the funeral, at the "residence near Midway." At the cemetery, the Masons took charge, and he was "buried with their customary rites."

The newspaper, like those of today, paid special attention to events with a local connection, and anything to do with St. Stephen's certainly merited attention. The third rector, who served during the war years, was the subject of a piece quoted on October 16th from the *Rome Bulletin*:

> Rev. George Macaulay, of Cartersville, officiated at St. Peter's Church on Sunday, Rev. George Wilson being confirmed to his bed by illness. Mr. Macaulay is one of the best and ablest ministers of the Diocese of Georgia, a faithful pastor, a devoted Christian, a friend and counselor of the lonely and humble, and a man without guile. Those who know him longest and most intimately admire . . . and love him best. May his visits to Rome be frequent.

The editor of the Milledgeville paper then added: "Truer and kinder words could not be spoken of any man. Mr. Macaulay is much beloved by many citizens of Milledgeville, where he was pastor of St. Stephen's Episcopal Church, many years."

Fortunately, weddings occurred to provide an offsetting to wait to the grief of funerals. The following appeared on November 13, 1883, under the heading "HYMNAL":

> On Wednesday afternoon at 4:00, St. Stephen's Episcopal Church in this city, was filled with and interested audience,

a symbol to witness the nuptials of Miss Nana Stoney of this city, and Mr. Charles Drake of Macon, formerly of Milledgeville. The impressive and beautiful ceremony was performed by the pastor, Rev. J. M. Stoney, a brother of the bride, who was, also, attended by another brother, Mr. C. L. Stoney, of Washington city, and Mr. Geo. D. Sanger, his partner in the drug business.

Description of the church expressed a scene that "was impressive and pleasing to the eye. Miss Ann Wright resided at the organ."

(A note should be made about the brother's hometown: The small town of Washington, Georgia, in Wilkes County, was founded before what might be regarded as its namesake, Washington D.C. During the nineteenth century, the Georgia town was referred to as Washington-Wilkes, while the national capital was called Washington City.)

A bit of unsettling news for St. Stephen's appeared in the December 4th issue of the Union & Recorder, regarding the departure of Captain J. W. Wilcox, though his connection with the church is not mentioned:

Capt. J. W. Wilcox has, we learn, resigned position of chief engineer at the asylum. This will be a great loss to the institution. His services in this position for years have been invaluable to the asylum. He has perfected the water and fire organization and been serviceable in a great many other directions. He was devoted to his work, and his labors and skill are everywhere to be seen in and about the institution. The captain, we understand, leaves purely because he can do better elsewhere, and does not think the state could afford to pay him the money he can make in another situation. He will [illegible] to Macon, and he knew enough to render assistance to the one who succeeds him, in the case of necessity.

Friends of Capt. Wilcox did not let him leave Milledgeville without

a proper sendoff, as recorded on January 22, 1884, under the
heading "AT THE OLD HOMESTEAD":

> Friday last was an ugly day, out and out, but there was a
> silver lining to the dark clouds, and the general discomfort
> out of doors. And it was the gathering of the friends of Dr.
> Thomas H. Kenan and mother and family in the old
> homestead, so well known to our citizens as the residence, in
> his prime, of Col. Augustus H. Kenan, a man who, while he
> lived, was always in the lead. The occasion that brought so
> many people together was a complement to Capt. J. W.
> Wilcox, late chief engineer at the asylum, that goes to Macon
> to invest his talents, his industry, and his capital in a business
> in which we sincerely wish him all success. He is a gentleman
> greatly beloved, and this entire community bid (sic) him
> goodbye with regret. In a notice of a private, social reunion,
> such as the one we have alluded to above, it would not be in
> good taste to make personal allusions, but, in behalf of his
> guests, in behalf of the entire company present, we rise to
> make our profoundest Salaam. It was one of those happy
> things a man sees now and then, in his pilgrimage, but, oh,
> how wide apart. There was dancing, and every good thing
> to eat and drink that the most sensitive stomach could crave.
> What more can I say?

The piece was signed with the initials J. H. N. Another tribute to
the man who had been called for Macon thirteen years previously
noted:

> We regret that this community has lost Capt. J. W. Wilcox.
> His commanding intelligence had . . . a large place in the
> social and religious life of Milledgeville. Macon has been
> able to make it to his pecuniary interest to remove there. We
> are glad of his increased prosperity.

Meanwhile, activities at St. Stephen's continued, as reported on

February 5, 1884, with the usual flowery praise of the bishop and his sermon:

> Bishop Beckwith confirmed a class of four at St. Stephen's Episcopal Church in this city on last Sabbath. Every seat in the church was filled and the services were interesting. At night the church was again filled to listen to the Bishop expound the Gospel . . . He was listened to with rapt attention, and rose at times to the sublimest heights of eloquence.

Elsewhere in that same edition, the editor was moved to comment, "If Bishop Beckwith was not in expander of Divine Law, what a superb tragedian he could make."

Needing funds, St. Stephen's sponsored a "Valentine Party and Fancy Dress Ball," announced in the next week's paper, February 12th. It would "be given at the Opera House, February 15th, commencing at 7 & 1/2 o'clock. Everybody cordially invited to attend. Young ladies and gentlemen, and children of all ages are requested to appear in costume, either fancy or comic. Comfortable seats provided for spectators." The "Committee of Arrangement" included "Mrs. C. P. Crawford, Mrs. A. Joseph, Mrs. G. T. Whilden, Mrs. Dr. Harris, Mrs. F. B. Mapp, Mr. P. J. Cline, Mr. A. Joseph, Mr. H. Turner, Mr. J. Miller, and Mr. W. S. Scott. The announcement concluded: "Admission 10¢. Oyster supper, sweetmeats and fruits will be served at low rates. Proceeds to be used for repairs upon the Episcopal Church." A follow-up story on February 19th, on a most successful evening, is headed "The Fancy Dress Carnival":

> Friday night last will long be remembered by the people of Milledgeville as the brightest, the prettiest, and pleasantest of all the glad enjoyed as evenings experience since the war. The Opera House parquette was crowded with "lookers on in Vienna," who composed the very flower of the city. The

rivers run."

Then follows a list of seventy-one young ladies "IN COSTUME—NO MASKS." Some came representing the "French princesses in the reign of Louis XV." The names of twenty-six gentlemen follow: Robin Hood, the Count of Monte Cristo, and a Laplander were represented. The editor's comments appear under the heading "side notes":

> The supper tables at the festival Friday night were superb, every good thing that could be provided for the palette was there in profusion and perfection. It was a very pretty unpleasant feature of the festival Friday night, the cordial cooperation of the ladies of all religious persuasions in the city. Though in the interest of the Episcopal Church peculiarly, the ladies of all the other churches assisted with cheerfulness and earnestness in making the affair a success.
>
> The festival netted over $200. The cake on Mrs. Judge White's table was a "gem" in its makeup. Mrs. DuBignon and Miss Rebecca Harris were very attentive to all their guests.

Thanks to the festival and many other money raising projects—all supported apparently not only by St. Stephen's parishioners but the entire town of Milledgeville—repairs were made to the church building.

Some information is appended to the history that Mrs. Furman wrote in 1877, signed by "W. W. Kimball" as rector:

> Mrs. Parish C. Furman gave $500 to the parish early in the year 1884, other subscriptions were added by many members

of the parish, and the church building was altered by removing the flat roof and replacing it with a Gothic roof; building a vestibule; re-weatherboarding the building, and other changes. When the contemplated alterations are completed it is expected that the building will be virtually new and much enlarged.

He also numbered the communicants at sixty-six as of July 1, 1884.

One twentieth-century historian termed the work done to the building as "the most drastic reconstruction and renovation, leaving it in the same style and form which remains almost a century later." He also credits Mrs. Furman with being "the largest donor" to the project. (Bonner, *St. S*). The paper gave almost no details in its report on February 26, 1884: "A new building has been erected right over the old Episcopal Church. It will soon be completed and, it is said, will be one of the handsomest houses of worship in the city." No mention is made in that brief report of the work of the much loved and recently departed Capt. Wilcox, who had begun work ten years previously to restore "the furniture of the chancel lost in the invasion of 1865." Thus reads, in part, a plaque still visible at the end of the altar rail near the organ. The full description follows:

> To the Glory of God, Captain John W. Wilcox, Vestryman of St. Stephen's Church, Restored the furniture of the chancel, Lost in the invasion of 1865, Over a period of ten years, He made of walnut Lectern, Litany Desk, Altar Rail, Table and Cross, Bishop's Chair-Priest's Chair, Pedestal for front Credence Table, Frame for Choir loft. 1874-1884

Mr. And Mrs. L.W. Anderson gave St. Stephen's a picture of Capt. Wilcox, who was born in 1840 and died in 1920. On the back of the picture, a clipping has been affixed. What appears before "In Memoriam" is not legible, but the piece goes on to say: "Among the Confederate soldiers who recently passes into the Great Beyond is Capt. John W. Wilcox, and surely none was more loyal to the

South, its traditions, and its people." The extent of his loyalty is
recounted:

> Often I have heard him say that if he was not permitted to
> go into heaven, he hoped he would be allowed to enter into
> whatever place the Army of Northern Virginia now occupied.

That loyalty, however, was not limited to the South: "Captain
Wilcox, although intensely Southern, was all-American also." The
memorial goes on to give an account of his forefathers, followed by
a brief biography and an account by a comrade in arms in the
Army of Northern Virginia. Unfortunately, nowhere in the lengthy
memorial is his association with St. Stephen's mentioned.

Whenever the Rev. Mr. Stoney spoke, he apparently drew an
appreciative crowd. On March 4, 1884, the Union & Recorder
carried an account one of his lectures, part "of a series of lectures to
be delivered before the literary societies of the young ladies of the
G. M. & A. College." The account says:

> Mr. Stoney, in his attractive, piquant way, took the young
> ladies on an imaginary excursion to Athens, the beautiful
> home of ancient culture. So pleased were his fellow travelers
> with Mr. Stoney as director of their excursion that they
> would be delighted to have him map out their trip again . . .
> and explore further the city that can justly boast that she
> found a cultivation a feeble infant and nourished it till it
> became a mature man rejoicing in beauty and strength.

That same issue of the paper noted, "Rev. J. M. Stoney, rector of
St. Stephen's Church, Milledgeville, officiated at St. Philip's Church,
Atlanta, last Sunday."

As usual on Easter Monday, as reported in the Union &
Recorder on April 22nd, vestry members and convention delegates
were elected. One vacancy had occurred with the death of Farish
C. Furman. Again, W. H. Scott and J. W. Wilcox were returned as
senior and junior warden respectively—despite the fact that Capt.

Wilcox had presumably moved to Macon. Elected along with incumbent F. G. Grieve were W. W. Lumpkin, Hatch Turner, and John G. Thomas. F. G. Grieve was also named secretary and treasurer again. W H Scott, Hatch Turner, and W. W. Lumpkin were named "delegates to the next diocesan convention to assemble at St. Philip's Church, Atlanta, Georgia, 14th of May, next."

"Thanks of the vestry and parish were returned to Mrs. O. M. Cone, and Messrs. Samuel G. White and Willie Carr for aiding in the music Easter Sunday and rendering it beautiful."

On May 13, 1884, the Union & Recorder reported on a successful "May Festival and Coronation":

> The ladies and young Misses of the Episcopal Church had a May festival and coronation at Brake's Opera House last Friday evening. Little Miss Rosa Mapp was crowned queen and performed her part admirably, as did all who participated in the beautiful ceremonies . . . followed by the serving of ice cream, strawberries, cake and lemonade . . . the affair netted $75.00.

In the adjoining column, "the ladies of the Episcopal Church offer sincere thanks to the young people and children of other denominations who took part in 'The Forest Nymph'; also to parents and other friends . . . who assisted in crowning the festival with beauty and success." Under "Personal Mention" in the next week's issue, May 20th, the editor reports "Rev. J. M. Stoney attended the Episcopal Convention in Atlanta." Also in that issue appeared news that church members did not want to hear:

> RESIGNED—We learn that the Rev. J. M. Stoney, rector of St. Stephens Episcopal Church in this city, has resigned his charge, and will probably make Camden, S. C., his future home. Mr. Stoney, in addition to his pastoral duties in this city, was chaplain at the Lunatic Asylum, in both of which positions he was useful and dutiful. He is a gentleman of fine address, and possesses an enthusiastic nature that makes him very

successful in whatever he undertakes. We shall part with him
and his pleasant family with much regret, and wish him the
fullest fruition of his aspirations in his new home.

On May 27th, the editor again bemoaned the rector's resignation:

The community, especially the aged and the poor amongst
us, will lose, in the removal of Rev. J. M. Stoney, a friend,
who was a friend indeed. Few men, since the removal of
Rev. C. W. Lane to Athens, have done as much as Mr. Stoney
has here . . . He visited the sick, cheered the desponding
(sic), and assisted the poor as far as his means would authorize.

On June 24th, the beloved rector's departure was fast approaching:

THE PARTING—Rev. J. M. Stoney, who for so many years
has been the faithful pastor of St. Stephen's Church in this
city, will remove to this new field of labour and next week.
His last sermon, as rector of this Church, will be preached
next Sunday morning. As soon as commencement is over,
he will remove it with his family to Camden, S.C., having
been announced to begin his work as rector of the Episcopal
Church in that place on the first Sabbath in July. He will be
greatly missed, not only by his church and congregation,
but by our whole community. May the blessings of Heaven
rest upon him and his, is the earnest prayer of all our people.

Note this official July 1st letter from the vestry to the departing
rector:

To all whom it May Concern:

The Rev. J. M. Stoney, having served this church and parish
for the past eleven years, and now leaves the same for other
fields of labor, we the vestry of St. Stephen's Church and
Parish, Milledgeville, Ga., deem it our duty to give him this

letter, that it may show his standing, and high esteem, and entertained for him by those with whom he parts. Mr. Stoney has performed all the duties devolving upon him, both as Priest and Pastor, to the entire satisfaction of his Parish. He has administered in Holy things with a fidelity seldom known. He has consecrated our people in faith, he has baptized the children in Holy baptism; he has visited the sick, prayed with the dying, he has buried our dead. The vestry undoubtably was expressing the feelings of all the communicant said. The letter continues:

In all these sacred offices he has been faithful, and the part with him, with heavy hearts, with a feeling of sadness and sorrow. But wherever his lot may be cast to all Vestries and Parishes, we the Vestry of St. Stephen's Church, Milledgeville, Ga., cheerfully commend him to their most favorable consideration.

It is signed by the two wardens, W. H. Scott, senior warden, and J. W. Wilcox, junior warden; F. G. Grieve, H. Turner, W. W. Lumkin, J. G. Thomas, Committee, and attested to by F. G. Grieve, secretary. It is unknown why the Rev. J. M. Stoney ran an announcement in the issue for July 11 stating, "Bishop Beckwith will not hold a confirmation in St. Stephen's Church next Wednesday night, as was announced last Sunday morning." Immediately below it is another announcement concerning the church: "The teachers and children of St. Stephen's Episcopal Church Sunday school will meet at 5:00 next Sunday afternoon, instead of in the morning. Mr. W. W. Lumpkin will preside." [Note the different spellings of the latter's name on July 8th and July 11th.] Another tribute to F. C. Furman, on July 29th, contained the editor's lament over missing "the memorial services, during the recent session of Baldwin Superior Court." The first item under "Personal Mention" in the July 29th issue reads:

NOTICE—The congregation of St. Stephen's Parish are urgently requested to meet in the Episcopal Church,

Wednesday, 30th, at 5:00 p.m. it is honestly hoped that each member of this congregation, old and young ladies, and gentlemen, young men and maidens, will be present on this occasion to attend to some important business in which they are all equally interested.

Left once more without a rector, St. Stephen's again was forced to depend upon substitutes. The paper took notice of one in the August 19th issue: "On Sunday last the Rev. C. J. Wingate from St. Paul's Church, Macon, Ga., held services, preached and administered the communion, in St. Stephen's . . . The church was crowded."

Evidently the congregation appreciated having a guest priest:

The congregation of St. Stephen's Church and Parish, are greatly indebted, to Mrs. Wright Bell, Miss Mattie Briscoe, and Mr. Samuel G. White for aiding so much by their sweet singing in rendering of the services and beautiful on Sunday last, 17 inst., and the vestry take this method to thank them for the same.

The "Personal Mention" column on September 23rd carried two sad items for St. Stephen's: "We are sorry to hear that Mrs. J. M. Stoney is very ill at her home in Camden, S. C . . . Capt. Wilcox's family left for their new home at Macon, on Wednesday last. We regret to lose such a family." On October 14th, notice was given of the return of the former rector:

RELIGIOUS NOTICE—The Rev. J. M. Stoney will preach and administer the Holy Communion in St. Stephen's Episcopal Church on Sunday, the 19th of October, 1884. All are invited to come. Pews free.

(One wonders regarding the last reminder; pews had been free for years.)

That same month brought more good news on October 16th:

"The many friends of Mrs. J. M. Stoney will be pleased to learn that she has so far recovered from per late severe illness as to be able to visit this city." Two more happy items appeared on October 21st: "We had the pleasure of meeting Rev. J. M. Stoney on Friday. He will probably remain here for a month . . . Mrs. Stoney, wife of Rev. J. M. Stoney, we are pleased to say, is improving in her health, which has recently been feeble."

The issue for October 21ˢᵗ carried the following, which indicates further the affection of people in Milledgeville for the former rector: "Rev. J. M. Stoney conducted services at St. Stephen's Church last Sabbath, and they were very interesting. The sermon was a fine one, and the church could not accommodate all who desire to enter it."

Sadly, Mrs. Stoney did not recover. The following appeared on November 4, 1884, under the heading "DEATH OF MRS. STONEY":

> Mrs. Alice Stoney, wife of Rev. J. M. Stoney, died at the residence of Mrs. F. C. Furman, last Sunday night. A few months ago Rev. Mr. Stoney resigned directorship of St. Stephen's Episcopal Church in this city, which position he held for many years, to accept a call at Camden, S.C., and he moved his family thither. Mrs. Stoney, from all along that residence in this city, where she made so many warmly attached friends, and had formed so many pleasant associations, was loath to give them up, and parted from them with sorrow. Soon after reaching her new home she was prostrated with a fever, and became dangerously ill, for some time, and often expressed a desire to return to Milledgeville. As soon as she was able to travel Mr. Stoney brought her here, fondly hoping that old associations being revived, she would improve in health and get entirely well. But this hope was not to be realized. Seeming to improve, after two weeks sojourn in the city with Mrs. F. B. Mapp, she was carried to the residence of Mrs. Furman on Friday last, where she died on Sunday night.

One week later, on November 11th, the paper reported:

> The funeral services of Mrs. J. M. Stoney, on Tuesday, at the
> Episcopal Church were largely attended. The church was
> crowded so the numbers had to leave, there not being even
> standing room. They were conducted by Rev. Mr. Wingate
> of Macon. The remains were buried in our city cemetery.

Despite deaths, life does go on, and it did so at St. Stephen's. On
December 9th, the paper carried the following announcement:

> BISHOP BECKWITH will preach at St. Stephen's Church
> in this city, on Sunday, December 21st, a "sermon to young
> men." The public are respectfully invited to attend,
> particularly the young men of the community. The Bishop
> will also confirm on that day any who wish confirmation.
> Candidates will please notify any member of the vestry.

Note a report on December 23rd, with the bishop's named
misspelled:

> Bishop Beckworth delivered his admirable sermon to young
> men, last Sunday at the Episcopal Church, in this city, and
> administered the rite of confirmation to a class of three
> persons. We wish every young man in the city could have
> been present and heard that sermon, but the day it was
> inclement, and the gunmen were conspicuous, only, by
> their absence on this interesting location.

We in the twenty-first century wish the editor had been more
explicit as to the content of the bishop's sermon. What did he say
that "every young man in the city" should have heard?

During the first half of 1885, without the Rev. Mr. Stoney or
another rector as deeply involved in community affairs, apparently
nothing went on at St. Stephen's or in the church at large to merit

attention from the newspaper. Bishop Beckwith, however, was still worthy of notice. The following appeared on March 3, 1885:

> Bishop Beckwith in his pastoral letter to the clergy of this Diocese says, when you hear the church bells ringing, remembered it is a call to prayer; if you cannot go to public prayer still you can't pray; and your counting rooms, on the wharves, wherever you may be, and whatever may be your engagement, you can lift your soul to God, confess your sins to Him, implore pardon, and asked for strength and guidance-thus we many have a Lenten service everywhere. "Pray without ceasing."

The appointment of "delegates to attend the 63rd annual convention of the Diocese of Georgia, to be held in Christ Church, Macon, Ga., May 6th, 1885" was reported on April 21st: "Wm. H. Scott, Hatch Turner, W. W. Lumpkin."

The following appeared on June 16th to announce the return to the area of a former rector of St. Stephen's: "We are pleased to learn from the *Madisonian*, that the Episcopal Church has secured the services of Rev. Geo. McCaulay bill has assumed charge of Advent parish and will soon move his family to that place." The Rev. Mr. McCauley had served St. Stephen's during the war years, 1861-65.

Although Professor Bonner's short history of St. Stephen's gives 1884 as the year the Rev. Mr. Stoney successor arrived, items in the Union & Recorder indicate otherwise. The calling and subsequent rival of a new record was noted several times. The edition of July 7, 1885, carried two paragraphs in different columns: "Rev. Richard W. Anderson has accepted a call to the pastorship of St. Stephen's Church (Episcopal) of this city and will hold his first service on Sunday, 12th instant."

The following also appeared in that issue:

> RELIGIOUS NOTICE—The vestry take pleasure in announcing to the public, that the Rev. Richard W. Anderson,

of Louisville, Kentucky, has accepted a call to St. Stephen's Episcopal Church, Milledgeville, Ga., and will hold his first service on Sunday, the 12ᵗʰ of July.

The vestry was apparently still trying to overcome any negative results of previous pew rentals, for it added this notice: "Pews free—all are invited to attend July 7ᵗʰ, 1885."

In one column of the next week's paper, readers were informed that some "Rev. Richard W. Anderson, the new rector of St. Stephen's Episcopal Church has arrived in this city." Readers were given even more personal information that most certainly would not be revealed today: "He is a young man and weighs 245 pounds." Evidently the editor had gone to observe him at his first service and liked what he heard, for another column reported that

> Rev. Richard W. Anderson, the new rector of St. Stephen's Church, held his first service last Sunday morning. A large congregation was present, and listened to an able and earnest sermon from the text: "I can do all things through Christ which strengthens me." The sermon made a fine impression.

The following week, on July 21ˢᵗ, readers were informed that "Rev. Rich'd W. Anderson has rooms at the St. Stephen's rector and takes his meals in the Mansion." The former governor's mansion had been transferred to Georgia Military College and was being used to house the dining room for the cadets.

Some indication of the importance of the organ and music to St. Stephen's is given in the following on August 4, 1885:

> Several members of the congregation of St. Stephen's Episcopal Church, have presented Mrs. E. E. Bell with a set of solid silver teaspoons, in a beautiful case, accompanied by a card containing the names of the donors. Mrs. Bell was formally organist of St. Stephen's Church, and sends her resignation has kindly led the music until arrangements could be made for supplying her place . . . This present is tendered

as a slight token of appreciation of her talent as a musician and her voluntary service since the arrival of the new rector.

Regardless of who was serving as rector, the ladies continued their activities, frequently some innovative social the event to raise money, the latest being "a Dickens' party." Readers were notified on October 6th:

> The ladies of the Episcopal Church will have a Dickens Party on Friday night, October 16th. The public are cordially invited to attend. They request as many ladies, gentlemen and children as possible to appear in costume to represent some character from Dickens, and carry out as far as they can the character they represent.

Citizens of Milledgeville, or at least subscribers to the Union & Recorder, were obviously expected to be familiar with the works of one of England's most popular nineteenth-century novelists. The announcement points out, "There will be no invitations issued except through the paper, and those who cannot appear in costume will find it quite amusing as spectators." No mention is made here of any cost. That and other pertinent information is contained in two paragraphs appearing on October 13th, when the ladies organization is also named:

> THE DICKENS PARTY to be given by the Ladies' Aid Society, next Friday night, October 16th, at the Amusement Hall, will be very enjoyable. All are invited to be present. No dancing, but many amusing features.
>
> Those in costume will please assemble in the dressing rooms on each side of the stage. The characters will be announced promptly at 7 1/2 o'clock. No one admitted on the floor except those in costume. Added inducement was "an elegant supper . . . for all who wish it. Admittance at the door, 10¢.

The "elegant supper" was followed by another death in the parish. The obituary for Mrs. Dr. Clarke appeared on November 24, 1885, with the headline identifying her as usual by her husband's title.

Mrs. Mamie Gesner Clark, who was 29, had only recently married Dr. Henry M. Clarke, "who had recently settled here and obtained a good practice as a dentist." The editor listed her many admirable attributes and the fact that she had "Lost her mother when she was very beyond and she had been chiefly reared in this place under the walleyes and tender care of her grandmother, Mrs. Fanny A. Herty." The editor notes that she was "a consistent member of the Episcopal Church and an active and faithful in the discharge of her religious duties."

No reader would hardly miss an announcement on March 9th, 1886, enlarged, bold type, of "Lenten Services at St. Stephen's Church, Milledgeville Georgia, Rev. R. W. Anderson, Rector." The Ash Wednesday service, with sermon, would be held at 11:00 a.m., with those on other weekdays at 4:00 p.m., until Good Friday, when the service would again be at 11:00 a.m. Also, Holy Communion would be celebrated "every Sunday until Easter." Then follows a "Prayer for Lent," by M. P. (sic) Whittingham.

The edition of May 4th carried the usual announcement of the vestry election on Easter Monday. W. H. Scott remained senior warden, but W. W. Lumpkin, an incumbent replaced Capt. Wilcox as junior warden. F. G. Grieve, Hatch Turner, J. G. Thomas, Thos. C. White, were all returned as vestrymen and Grieve as secretary-treasurer. A long piece by C. Sharp and dated April 28, 1886, also appeared on May 4th, with portions of difficult to read. He begins by identifying himself only as "a temporary sojourner in the historic old city of Milledgeville" which he calls a "quaint old city, grand in its own time, with its long the breaches of stretching, patriarchal elms, its grassy slopes and undulating beauty, many thrilling memories of the city, its old Capitol, with its embrasure parapets and castelled walls, broad faces, and its Old Executive Mansion, and with all its archives embalmed in the hearts of all, . . . a dear spot to every Georgian." Now he brings up St. Stephen's, which had certainly impressed this "temporary sojourn":

> It was my pleasure to attend Easter services at St. Stephen's Church on Sunday last, where were many charming evidences of their intellectual taste and culture, in the beautiful handiwork of the noble Christian ladies, in the ornamentation of the church with spring flowers, emblems and mottoes, appropriate to the joyous and festive occasion . . . The chancel arch was beautifully ornamented with a graceful wild smilax, from the center of which was suspended a floral Cross, with a similar one of pure white roses resting upon each pilaster, half concealed by the intricate tracery of the lines, while be needed, across the arch, was stretched aloft white letters on a scarlet background the appropriate sentence, "The Lord is Risen."
>
> The organ loft, chancel rail, the windows, doors and chandeliers were also decorated with the same graceful and roses, and among which bloomed bright spring flowers, not "wasting their sweetness on the desert air," but shedding a rich beauty and sweet perfume over a very appreciative congregation.
>
> Inside the chancel whale, the decorations were exceptionally beautiful and appropriate. Upon the altar, was a cross 3 ft. high, of choice roses bordered with green, rising from a (?) of this note Bowles, spotted with rich,(orange?) Pansies. Honesty and, near the bishops share, was another handsome floral Cross, while the chair itself seemed a perfect bower of smilax and flowers. The baptismal font was radiant with geranium blossoms of all shades; the lectern cover bore, on its front, a pure white star, composed entirely of white cleve (sic) pinks, and upon the bearer' and linen cloth' of the altar, (?) out, in glittering silver the great characters 'Alpha' and 'Omega', indicating that expression found in Revelations (sic) first chapter and (?) verse. Above one of the side windows in fancy cut silver letter, was the sentence,

"THOU ART MY SON," and opposite, and like characters,
the words "CHRIST OUR PASSOVER."

Rev. Mr. Anderson, the able Rector, delivered an earnest
and impressive sermon on the resurrection. The choir of
trained voices, led by Mrs. Newell, with Mrs. Farish Furman
presiding at the organ, tendered the Te Deum and other
chants in fine style, and altogether, the service, with its
appropriate surrounds, a was instructive, pleasing and
comforting in the extreme, to a congregation so large that
every available space was filled, while many who could not
get even standing room, turned away to attend other services.

As the services were ended and the congregation turned
to be part, they beheld over the door through which they
had entered, and what had hitherto been unobserved,
because behind them, the partying and earnest benediction
of the church—the words "PEACE BE WITH YOU."

Kindly ever yours,
C. Sharp.
Milledgeville, Ga., April 28th, 1886"

Just as Bishop Elliott had earned the respect of Milledgeville editors,
so had Bishop Beckwith. The Union & Recorder also recognized
the importance of Episcopalians in the state's life, for on October
12, 1886, it devoted several inches to a tribute from the Bishop
despite the fact that he was eulogizing the senior warden of Christ
Church in Macon, the late Colonel Lewis N. Whittle.

Marriages continued to provide happy news offsetting that of
deaths. The wedding of Mr. Joseph W. Smith of Burke County "to
Miss Ida Dowsing of this city" was reported in the issue for
November sent. It had taken place "on Tuesday evening blast at
half past 8 o'clock . . . at the Episcopal Church, the rector Rev. R.
W. Anderson officiating." The usual long account follows. The
church was so filled with ladies that "a few gentlemen only occupied
seats, while a number of them down standing in the rear of the
pews—the Church being in fact crowded with people." The

organist for the occasion is identified as Miss Fannie Stembridge with "the Rev. Mr. Anderson, clothed in his clerical vestments" reading "the beautiful and impressive marriage service of the Episcopal Church." The church itself was described as being "tastefully ornamented with flowers wrought into sundry pretty devices, among which, suspended from the chandelier, was a handsome arrangement of flowers exhibiting in a monogram the letters D and S, the initials of the surnames of the bride and groom." As if anyone were likely to forget the denomination, the editor added near the end, "We should have mentioned sooner that the bride was 'given away' after the Episcopal custom, by her brother, Mr. Charlie Dowsing." In the adjoining column of the paper, further evidence is given of the respect held for the previous rector:

> Rev. J. M. Stoney, for a number of years the esteemed pastor
> of the Protestant Episcopal Church in Milledgeville, was
> expected to preach at the asylum chapel last night. Mr.
> Stoney, deservedly (and without reference to creeds) has a
> great many friends in this locality.

The observance of Easter in 1887 at St. Stephen's was noted first on March 29th, under the heading "Easter festival":

> The superintendent and teachers of St. Stephen's Sunday
> School are making preparation for a very enjoyable festival
> for the Sunday School scholars to take place on an afternoon
> of Easter Sunday, which occurs on April 10th, this coming
> Sunday week.

(Notice the use of the expression "this coming Sunday week," rather than "a week from Sunday.") Obviously St. Stephen's had established a firm reputation for Easter services because the piece continues:

> It is universally the case that on every Easter, the little church
> is crowded to its utmost capacity and from the preparations
> we hear they are making, the services for this Easter A and

the decorations of the church when will be the most pleasing for years past and it is supposed that quite a large assemblage will be in attendance.

The follow-up story appeared on April 12th under the heading "Easter at St. Stephen's." Given the size of the parish, one might be led to think that the congregation was made up of non-parishioners:

> At an early hour, the seats in Little St. Stephen's (Episcopal) Church began to fill, and by half past 10, the time the previously announced for service to began, all the seats were occupied, chairs filled all the aisles and every available inch of standing room even was filled with an interested congregation.

There follows the usual detailed description of the decorations. It is heartening to know that the laity were involved in one of the major festival days, even with the rector present: "Mr. W. W. Lumpkin, recently appointed late reader for the parish, read the service, and Rev. R. W. Anderson, the Rector, delivered a short but impressive sermon." The editor cited "want of time at this late hour "for preventing "a minute description of the beautiful evolutions of the pupils" in the afternoon Easter Festival of the Sunday school. The editor concluded, "Altogether both services were enjoyed by a very large attendance."

It apparently did not take the Rev. Mr. Anderson long to establish credit with merchants. A thoughtful citizen, Alice Andrews, has provided St. Stephen's with a business card on which he ordered groceries: "T. E. White & Company will deliver to bearer one small sack of flour & why it pounds of meat and charge same to my account. April 2, 1877." It is signed R. W. Anderson. Alas for St. Stephen's, he elected not to continue his tenure much longer, for according to the Union-Recorder on July 19th, "Rev. R. W. Anderson, rector of St. Stephen's Episcopal Church in this city has resigned his charge, and will leave this week." No explanation is given for either the resignation or sudden departure.

"The Rev. F. Harriman Harding, Rector 1924-1954, with choir"

"The Rev. John J. Lanier, Rector 1899-1907"

"Madrigal at St. Stephens"

"Mrs. Bland, Organist, whose daughter Nylic, decades after the Civil War, helped bring a happy ending to the sad story of the pouring of molasses into the organ pipes during the Union Army's occupation of the church"

"The Historic Sanctuary, St. Stephens"

"An Antebellum Rector:
The Rev. Judson Morris Curtis, Rector, 1859-1861"

"The Pulpit of St. Stephens"

"Window in Memory of Mrs. Fannie Joseph"

"Window Dedicated in Memory of The Rev. J.M. Stoney,
Rector, 1873-1884"

"Mr. Ken Shermer, Senior Warden and Chief Verger, with
The Rev. Judson Child, Seventh Bishop of Atlanta"

"The Rev. Edward Sellers, rector 1983-1988,
with Bill Eason and Ralph Green"

"Inez Hawkins, first woman to serve as junior and senior
warden, with The Rev. Milton Murray, Rector, 1964-1970"

"Mr. Frank Davis, long standing member of St. Stephens, with The Rev. Milton Murray, Rector, 1964-1970, and The Rev. Dr. C.K. Robertson, Rector, 1999-present.

As has been mentioned, the Union-Recorder liked all kinds of local news. Therefore it must have welcomed a short history of Baldwin County by a writer identified only by the initial "N," perhaps observing his 50th year in Milledgeville. The piece of appeared on July 19, 1887 under the heading "Baldwin County-Milledgeville." "N" reports:

> This County was purchased of the Creek Indians, in 1802, and extended as high as High Shoals on the Appalachee River. Courts were held for sometime in Hillsboro (now in Jasper County) where there were a few houses and one dram shop. In the year 1828, the south part of the county produced extensive and fine crops of sugar cane; the same land today would produce equally fine specimens if more attention was bestowed on the cultivation of that valuable crop.

With no transition, the writer identifies "Abraham Baldwin, for whom the county was named." A graduate of Yale College, he "was one of the founders of Franklin College (now the University of Georgia) in 1783. He was a Senator in Congress, helped to form the Federal Constitution, and died in Washington City in 1807." The writer then continues with the history of Milledgeville, which . . .

> Was laid off by act of the legislature passed in 1803, when Louisville was the Seat of Government. The first building erected here was of logs, and built in 1804 on Franklin Street. The first frame house was built by Gen. John Scott in 1805, and was standing on the corner of Franklin and Elbert streets when the writer of these lines came here in 1837 and for many years after. The principal business of the town was done on these streets for many years . . . The old Capitol building was erected in 1828 at a cost of $115,000. The clock in the cupola cost $1,000. The Legislature held its

first session in Milledgeville in 1807. The original State
House was burned . . .

He gives no date. As he continues, instead of the correct date of
1803 for the constitution of Milledgeville by the Legislature, he
gives . . .

> December, 1836, with a Mayor and six Aldermen, just as it
> has now. For many years steamboats came up only to the
> locks, one mile and half below the city, where there were
> large cotton warehouses, and houses for the storage of goods,
> which were hauled to the city in wagons. Nichols and
> Deming at that time did the principal Grocery business in
> the city. When the locks were entirely completed, the
> steamboats came up to the bridge, just opposite the city . . .
> We have taken some pains to prepare this brief account of
> the early history of our county and the city of Milledgeville,
> and our readers here would do well to preserve it for ready
> reference. I may continue these sketches, with more
> particularity, from 1837 to 1887.

Death paid no attention to the lack of a priest at St. Stephen's. The
obituary of Lewis Dowsing was carried on August 16th. A young
man of "only about twenty-one years of age" he died from "what is
called 'Typho-Malarial Fever'" shortly after moving to Macon, where
he was employed. His funeral was "held at the Episcopal church
by the Rev. Mr. Winchester of Macon," and he was buried "in our
community cemetery."

Although the name of the "Rev. John Moncure of Gallipolis,
Ohio," is not listed by Professor Bonner, the Union-Recorder had
learned on September 13, 1887, that he "has been called to the
rectorship of St. Stephen's Episcopal church in this city."

Efforts to involve the community in support for St. Stephen's
continued. The following appeared on October 18: "There was a
supper and a pleasant entertainment at the Amusement Hall last

Friday evening, proceeds for the benefit of Episcopal Church." Voted "the most popular lady present," Miss May Bond was given "a handsome cake." Several weeks later, as reported on November 22nd:

> There was a very pleasant Musicale on Tuesday evening by members of St. Stephen's Episcopal Church in this city. The company present was highly entertained by the instrumental and vocal performances of Misses Stembridge, Olive Herty, Laura Paine and Minnie Bellamy. A recitation by Miss Hattie Henderix was greatly enjoyed.

With no mention as to why the Rev. Mr. John Moncure failed to answer the call to St. Stephen's, the Union & Recorder announced on December 13th, "We are pleased to learn that the Episcopalians of this city have secured the services of Rev. H. J. Broadwell, as Rector of St. Stephen's church. He was formerly of South Carolina, but now of Fonda, N.Y. He is expected to arrive here today, with his family, a wife, and one child, and will preach next Sabbath. We unite with the Episcopalians, and our citizens generally, in extending them a cordial welcome.

Some obituaries, including that for Mrs. Adolph Joseph on December 20, were being shortened, though the language did not change:

> On Tuesday morning last, our community was startled by the intelligence of the death of this well known and estimable lady, which event took place at 8 a.m., December 13th, at her residence in this city.

A long paragraph still provides a rather full description of her and her attributes. The last paragraph not only gives time and place of the funeral but also lists pall-bearers. Services "were held on Wednesday afternoon at the Episcopal church, and were conducted by Rev. Mr. Broadwell, rector. Not withstanding the extremely inclement weather, there was a very large attendance."

Rectors came and went at St. Stephen's, but Bishop Beckwith remained a constant in the life of the church and diocese. The Union-Recorder included a brief paragraph on January 17, 1888, under the heading "From our Exchanges": "Bishop Beckwith's forthcoming book of travels is awaited with much interest." On April 24th, his activities were reported in a piece picked up from the *Macon News*: "During Bishop Beckwith's recent visit to Macon he was the guest of Rev. Mr. Powers, Rector of St. Paul's. We are pleased to state that the Bishop's health has been greatly improved by his trip across the waters to the Holy Land." There is then a recapitulation of the Bishop's confirmation activities, with 65 confirmed from four churches in the Macon area.

On May 1st, the Union-Recorder reported, "The marriage of two popular young people, Mr. R. W. Roberts and Miss Marwood Herty took place last evening at the Episcopal church. Mr. Roberts is one of our rising young lawyers, and is fortunate in having won the heart and hand of so charming a young lady." The same issue carried a one-paragraph announcement that Bishop Beckwith had "arrived in the city on Thursday afternoon and preached at St. Stephen's church that night." In an adjoining column, it was reported that "a class of thirteen were confirmed by Bishop Beckwith on Thursday night last. The Bishop gave a deeply interesting account of his recent visit to the Holy Land." Again the editor cound not resist the temptation to laud the Bishop's eloquence. Those confirmed were listed as "Misses Laura Belle Paine, Lizzie B. Stembridge Etta Miller, Leonora Ellen Perry, Mary Eleanor Brown, Jennie Americus Tollison, and Mrssrs. Frank Herty, O'Hara Fox, Arthur McCulloch, James M. Wilkes, Henry J. Perry, Hansell W. Compton, Rufus W. Roberts." Later that month, on the 22nd, the Union-Recorder printed what must be virtually all of the Bishop's "annual address at the Diocesan Convention last week at Augusta."

The first notice of repairs to St. Stephen's, soon to be undertaken, came on June 26th, with the following announcement of the formation of what amounted to a building fund committee, though with a far more engaging name:

> The congregation of St. Stephen's Episcopal Church feeling very much the need of repairs upon their church have formed themselves into an organization called Cheerful Workers. We each ne pledge ourselves to do certain work and to assist each other in every way possible. And we ask of the public generally that those who have any of the following work to be done to give us their aid.

A long list of projects which were expected to produce funds includes various aspects of cooking and needlework, while the list "To Sell" names even "Fantail pigeons." Officers that had been elected were named: "President, Mr. W. W. Lumpkin; Secretary, Miss Fannie Fuss; Treasurer, Mr. R.W. Roberts; Vice Presidents, Mr. W. H. Scott, Mr. Joseph Staley, Mr. H. Turner, Mrs. Robt. Whitfield, Mrs. F. C. Thurman, Mrs. R. W. Roberts, F. G. Grieve." Below was printed a "NOTICE" that "The Society of the Cheerful Workers will meet at the residence of Mr. F. B. Mapp, next Thursday afternoon promptly at 6:00 o'clock." Not only were all members of the parish invited, but "also those who are not members." It was pointed out that "all the other churches in this city are nicely fixed up now, except St. Stephen's, and if each one of us will do our duty, we too, will not feel ashamed of ours." Of course those who preferred to give money rather than time and/or talents were encouraged to do so: "A freewill offering of adjust any amount that they feel they can give each month." The same announcement of the formation of the Cheerful Workers committee was printed again on July 3rd and July 10th.

Despite the efforts of the congregation to make improvements at St. Stephen's, they were soon at without a rector again, apparently with note advance warning. The following paragraph appeared on July 17: "Rev. A. J. Broadwell left last Thursday for his home in Connecticut. He will not

return, and at St. Stephen's Church is again without a rector."
That same week, the Bishop was back in the news, having been
quoted, "The fires of intemperance would soon die out if we
could only save the children." Evidently that temperance
movement still lived.

Who knows what prompted the editor to begin on November
27, 1888, what was apparently intended as a series of "Brief Local
Pen Pictures of Living Men." Headed "Kind Words from 'Uncle
Bob'," who was not further identified, the first featured the man
Joseph Staley, elected mayor of Milledgeville the previous January,
though he was not identified as such in the story until halfway
through it. The last paragraph does not mention St. Stephen's but
merely says that he "is an Episcopalian," married with a married
daughter and grandchildren. St. Stephen's could rest easy that "he
has no desire to return to Old England."

Spelling bees certainly seemed popular in those days before
computers and an invention known as "spell check" took the place
of the well known Webster's speller. The year 1889 began with a
notice on January that a competition would take place that night
"at the courthouse [for the] benefit of the Episcopal Church," with
both "young ladies and gentlemen of Milledgeville" participating.
The notice continues:

> The admission fee is only 10¢, and a rich and rare treat
> Kuwait all who attend. What fun there will be listening to
> gray-haired sires recall old memories of the Webster's "Blue
> Back," as they spell side by side with lads of the more modern
> schools.

Clearly in 1889 our ancestors were much more easily entertained,
not to mention much more inexpensively, than we are today. A
writer identified as "C. SHARP" wrote a piece that appeared in
the January 22nd edition of "one of the most enjoyable defense for
some time past . . . the spelling bee at the courthouse, last Friday
night, for the benefit of St. Stephen's Episcopal church. However

simple the entertainment may seem to us, it attracted the elite of
the city:

> Col. Miller Grieve and Hon. W. W. Lumpkin tossed up
> heads or tails for the first choice, or first pick . . . and
> proceeded to choose alternately a speller from the audience,
> until they had caught in each class of fifteen, making thirty
> in all who were willing to test their orthography.

C. Sharp, noting that some of them were "old grey haired men"
declared what "a unique sight to see" them and "have grown cadets
and sweet little misses yet in their teens, all in the same spelling
Class." Further . . .

> There was no little amusement in many rounds of applause
> at the various excuses of those who were called upon, but
> declined to come forward and spell.

Professor Hill, who is not further identified, "from a selected list,
gave out the words to each member in succession of each class
alternately, while Dr. I. L. Harris with a Webster unabridged
dictionary in front of them acted as referee . . . The first to go
down was our genial and popular wholesale merchant, Capt. W. T.
Conn, who from over-anxiety, embarrassment or some other cause,
made a laughable blunder in 'red breast', putting the *ea* in 'red'
instead of in 'breast,' the U.S. spelling it out 'read brest'." C.
Sharp, using a Latin term meaning collapse of language, excuses
Capt. Conn further by saying the error "must have been simply a
lapsus linguae, but he went out very good naturedly, amidst a roar
of laughter and applause." Other errors, some obviously intended,
provoked further laughter. "Want of space," the readers were told,
"prevents following all the laughable and sometimes ridiculous
(sic) blunders that were made." One Mr. Hinkley, also unidentified,
won first prize, "a neat silver medal, made by Mr. Vallie Hafner,"
while Capt. Conn, being the first out, "can drink his consolation

out of the five cent tin cup, offered as the booby prize." As a final summary, C. Sharp notes:

> All good feeling prevailed and much merriment and pleasure, as well as a pretty fair sum considering the small price of admission, (only 10¢) was the result. We might very well enjoy it and other similar trade in the future.

The amount of funds produced for the church was not given. On January 22nd, the paper carried a brief paragraph informing readers that Bishop Beckwith was scheduled to "preach at the Episcopal Church in the city on Sunday, 27 January."

Also on January 22nd, attention was turned to another communicant of St. Stephen's, this time the secretary-treasurer, Rufus W. Roberts, who "joined the Episcopal Church" and was named to his position on the vestry a year later, "thereby showing his gratitude to God for the happiness that had crowned his young manhood, but promising to be governed by His laws."

A very short notice appeared on January 29th of the death of another parishioner of some years, Mrs. Henrietta Kenan, 82, "widow of the late Hon. A. H. Kenan" and mother of Dr. T. H. Kenan. She was a member of the Episcopal Church, but as there is no rector here at present, Reverends J. R. King, and D. McQueen officiated at the funeral services, which were held at the residence of Dr. T. H. Kenan on Friday afternoon." The adjoining column reports that "Bishop Beckwith was not able to be here last Sabbath. He will be present next Sunday, and holds services morning and evening at St. Stephen's Episcopal Church."

Sad news was brought to the parish on a February 5, 1889, when the paper reported the death of the third rector of St. Stephen's, the Irish—born Rev. Mr George Macaulay, who served 1851-56. After ill health for nearly two years, he died in Atlanta on the preceding Wednesday "of paralysis." The following day, at 12:30, "a large congregation assembled at St. Philip's Church to pay a last sad tribute. The services were conducted by Bishop

Beckwith, who referred to Mr. Macaulay's life as a bright one, full of devotion to the Master." The body of the deceased was brought by train to Milledgeville and "taken to the residence of Mrs. Fielding Lewis, the mother-in-law of the deceased." Inasmuch as St. Stephens had not called a new rector, Rev. D. McQueen of the Presbyterian Church officiated at the grave" on Friday morning.

Bishop Beckwith, according to the addition of February 5th, "preached at St. Stephen's Church in this city last Sunday to a large congregation." Once more reference is made to his eloquence: "If ever in the whole course of our life we listened to a more eloquent sermon it has faded from our memory. The Bishop is a wonderfully gifted orator. His argument is as sound as his diction is a beautiful."

Life for St. Stephen's parishioners went on outside the church. In their leisure, they were undoubtedly reading fiction in the tradition of American humor. Middle Georgia produced several of those authors and claims a native of Ohio, William Tappan Thompson. His works appeared in the *Madison Miscellany Journal,* which he edited. Milledgeville's own most famous writer, Flannery O'Connor, belongs to a later version of the tradition. One of the outstanding characters of such works is the use of words spelled more or less phonetically according to a local dialect.

The Union-Recorder, entering into the spirit of the location, printed a piece on February 12th with an explanatory sentence: "The following is a copy of a challenge cent for the Bee to be given next Friday night at the courthouse for the benefit of the Episcopal Church."

Miss _ _ _ _ _

Citie,

We thee undersined Wauking Dicktionaries off Milledgeville, Jauga, du herebye chalinge yu andyure fear sex toea mach game of spelling on Fridy evning, February 15th, at thee Kart Hous.

　　'Ech syde toe B composses off tweontie-foe members.
Mr. Hinkly wil knot spel, but giv out the wurds.

The names of twenty-four "Wauking Dicktionaries" then listed, followed by an equal number of ladies' names. The announcement concludes in standard English, giving the prizes:

> As the Bee will be over rather early, the Dummy (a local train) will be at the door at the close, and will make the trip to the asylum and back, enabling those who wish to take a ride before going home, an opportunity to do so. Charges will be as usual. Doors opened at 7 o'clock. Swinton's Word Book will be used. The best seller will be rewarded and elegant cake—the poorest, a large ginger cake.

Unfortunately, inclement weather called the spelling bee to be "postponed until this, Tuesday evening, 19th." The editor urges, "Let everybody attend." Despite the postponement, the addition of February 26th proclaimed the spelling bee to have been "well attended." Although one or two of the ladies and "many of the young men were wanting . . . Miss Olive Herty remained as the most successful" and won the advertised winner's cake.

Evidently a priest was visiting Milledgeville, for a paragraph in an adjoining column announced, "Services will be held at the Episcopal Church, Thursday night, 21st at 7:30 p.m. by Rev. Chaucy Williams of Augusta." The Bishop continued his visitations, one to Greensboro being recorded in the April 2nd issue, which also carried this unhappy news:

> The residence in Atlanta of Mrs. Lizzie Macaulay, widow of the late Rev. George Macaulay, was destroyed by fire last Thursday morning. The furniture and all the clothing of the family were consumed. The many friends of Mrs. Mccauley in this city sympathize with her in her misfortune.

Despite the lack of a rector or a visiting priest, Easter services at St. Stephen's were conducted, by a lay reader, W. W. Lumpkin, as reported on April 23rd. Further, the church was decorated "with good taste, profusely and becomingly." On May 26th, "all the members of the congregation of St. Stephen's Church are requested to meet at the church Sunday March 31st at 11 o'clock a.m.," though no reason is given.

Misfortune struck closer to home in June, when Miss Mary Herty died "on Monday night, after a lingering illness." she is identified in the account on June 18th as . . .

> a teacher in the preparatory Department of the Middle Georgia Military & Agricultural College for seven years, and was a most successful instructress of the young during her term of service. She was a member of St. Stephen's Episcopal Church in this city and it was deeply attached to its creed and its work. The funeral services on Tuesday afternoon were impressive.

Because St. Stephen's still lacked a rector, the service was "conducted by Rev. J. B. Winchester, of Macon."

Another visitation by Bishop Beckwith to St. Stephen's, this one "on Sunday, December 8th, at 11 a.m.," was noted on November 12th, with an unusual final sentence: "Services will be held in the church unless other notice is given." The reason for the uncertainty of the site of services is explained a week later, on November 19th:

> The improvements being made at St. Stephen's Episcopal Church will add greatly to the comfort of the congregation as well as add to the harmony of the external appearance of the building.

Perhaps the editor forgot, but in any event, he added, "We learned that Bishop Beckwith will soon visit the city and preach at St. Stephen's church." Or perhaps he was just reminding his readers, for another brief item on December 3rd also contains more information: "Bishop Beckwith will preach in this city and next Sunday. If the repairs and improvements on the Episcopal Church are not completed, the services will be held in the Methodist church." The repairs were obviously completed during the week, which produced more sad news for many Southerners, the death of the President of the Confederacy, Jefferson Davis, on December 6th, in New Orleans, Louisiana (Encyclopedia Britannica, VII, Williams, 85). The paper on December 10th noted that "the prayer of Bishop Beckwith at the Sunday morning services in St. Stephen's Church . . . for the family of ex-president Davis, touched deeply the hearts of his congregation.

Under the heading "Bishop Beckwith," and with no unity or coherence, the other item contains the usual high praise for the Bishop and also refers to repairs at St. Stephen's:

> This distinguished divine delighted our people by his presence and pulpit to utterances on last Sabbath at St. Stephen's Episcopal Church . . . The building has been greatly improved in the past few weeks. The bishop had a fine of audience and his sermon was one that impressed his intelligent audience. The little church didn't have standing room, but it had a heart to take all and will came to hear it the most eloquent man in Georgia in or out of the pulpit.

A would-be poet, "one of St. Stephen's flock" was inspired on December 2nd to compose "Verses to St. Stephen's Church," which appeared in the edition of December 17th and lamented the lack of services due to the repairs. The same issue also reported, "In closing a fine tribute to Mr. Davis at Atlanta last week Bishop Beckwith said, "Let us remember the example of his life." The Bishop called the late Confederate President "a child of God's Church—the incarnation of principle and the greatest exponent of duty performed for duty's sake." The final notice of 1889 pertaining to St. Stephens also appeared in that edition: "Rev. Mr. Kimball of Macon, held religious services at St. Stephen's church last Sunday." The Rev. W. W. Kimball added two paragraphs to Mrs. Furman's history, relating that "I became the rector January 12, 1889. I found the church in beautiful repair, interior."

☩ ☩ ☩

Then & Now: Although the nature of the events has at times changed, socials and fundraisers remain—as they have always been—a vital part to the life of the parish.

Giving a fresh twist to the tradition of the bazaars of a century past, recent years have led to the creation of the St. Stephen's Auction, an annual fall evening of fun, food and drink, and lots of items on which to bid. In "lean" years for the church, the money raised in the auction actually helped offset operating costs; in healthier times, the money has been earmarked for both parish outreach projects (such as Habitat for Humanity) and the Historic Building Preservation Fund. Faithful workers by the name of Blenk, Eason, Bowman, Farris, Crumbley, Zarkowsky, and many others, have for years made the annual auction an evening to which people throughout the community look forward with enthusiasm.

There have been other social events that have been successful, and well remembered, including dances, pancake suppers, lecture/teaching series, and concerts. Several years ago, in an attempt to raise funds and create a fresh and unique atmosphere of laugher, music, and great food, the Shrove Tuesday Low Country Boil came to be. Guests come to eat lots of shrimp and celebrate together the Mardi Gras tradition before the somber solemnity of the following day's Ash Wednesday services. Along with the auction and twice-a-year Jumble Sales, this helps provide even more income for parish outreach endeavors.

Much was said in the newspapers of old about the visits to Milledgeville of former diocesan bishops, whose presence and gifts were seemingly well appreciated by parishioners and city residents alike. In more recent decades, we have found relationships between bishops and rectors at times encouraging and at times strained. Yet even as the Rt. Rev. J. Neil Alexander took up the work of episcopal oversight inherited from Bishops Allen, Child, Sims—indeed from Stephen Elliott himself— so we find St. Stephen's once more in a position of cooperation and leadership with the diocese.

6

New Challenges: The 1890s

The Union-Recorder ran the following paragraph on January 7, 1890:

> Rev. W. W. Kimball, the new rector of St. Stephen's Episcopal Church, in this city, preached on Sunday morning and again at night. He originally came to Georgia from Virginia, but for three years just past he has served in Macon. The members of St. Stephen's are much pleased with their new rector.

A church historian lists him as one of "ten missionaries in addition to the Diocesan Missionary" being supported (Malone, 131).

On January 14th, under the heading "St. Stephen's Church, W. W. Kimball, Rector," readers were informed that "the Rector will officiate in St. Stephen's on the first, third, fourth, and fifth Sunday mornings and night, on second Sunday night, also every Wednesday night. Lay services second Sunday." The following week, readers were invited to "Come and here the subject explained," said subject to being "The St. Stephen's Church Guild," to be "organized on Wednesday night, and the church."

Once more the ladies of the church were busy with their projects, according to an item on January 21st when readers were urged to "Come one! come all! To ye opera hall Friday night and bring nickels bright to help Ye Ladies Aid Society of St. Stephen's Church; admission 25¢." College students and children were given a special price of a "15¢ Gallery 15¢." On January 28th a follow-up piece appeared with one of the first mentions of outreach:

> St. Stephen's Church Guild, an association for cooperative work for all interested in the church, was organized last week. In this guild all can (unreadable) a special work. The different chapters are known as Bishop's Salary, convention expenses, Diocesan sessions, for Strangers, for the sick and Sunday school.

The same issue carried a laudatory review of The Old Folks' Concern:

> Given by the Ladies Aid Society of St. Stephen's Church in this city, on Friday evening last. It was attended by a large audience who were delighted with the entire performance. It was unique, and exhibited a local musical talent that could not be surpassed by any city in Georgia of the size of Milledgeville . . . Taken all in all, it was one of the best shows seen in Milledgeville in months.

According to the editor, "The people of the city are anxious to have the concert repeated, and we learned that it will be before Lent, with some changes, which will make it more interesting." Again, he blames lack of space "to speak of the 'Old Folks Concert' fuller. But we can say that all was well done, and everyone present got fully a dollar's worth of amusement for 25 cents, besides the satisfaction of feeling that each had contributed something to very worthy cause." The cause was not identified, but the "net proceeds amounted to about $50," indicating an excellent turnout.

In another column, the Union-Recorder welcomed the Rev. Mr. Kimball:

> Rev. W. W. Kimball, rector of St. Stephen's Church in this city, is a pleasant gentlemen, and he promises to be a fine addition to our society as well as a most acceptable head of the Episcopal Church.

On the Sunday preceding February 11th, "Rev. Mr. Kimball, rector of St. Stephen's Episcopal Church, conducted services at Sparta."

As usual funerals took their, this one, reported on February 11, for a child:

> Tinsley Sewell, youngest child of Mrs. Mary Sewell, and grandson of Capt. Howard Tinsley, died last Friday night after a brief illness. He was a lovely child, four or five years of age. The of funeral services were conducted by Rev. Mr. Kimball, at the residence, 9 o'clock, Sunday morning.

Headlines were beginning to be used more and more in the Union-Recorder. One appeared elsewhere in the same issue of race story about "'Lenten services at St. Stephen's' on Wednesday February 19, 9:30 a.m. and 7:30 p.m. Thursday, 3:30 p.m.; Friday 7:30 p.m." The rector issued a "cordial welcome to all" . . . but did not mention free pews.

Although St. Stephens was not mentioned, a piece on the Lenten season, printed on February 20th, pointed out that it "is observed by the Catholics, the Episcopalians and Lutherans as a marked feast in the calendar, and by other denominations in a casual way."

The same issue advised readers of the missionary activity of the Diocese of Georgia with a report of a visit to St. Stephen's by the Rev. H. K. Rees, the diocesan evangelist, with "The object desired" being "to unite every baptized person of all ages been in active work to advance the missionary cause."

The Rev. Mr. Stoney may have severed his relationship bid St. Stephen's, but the lasting impression he made is indicated by the interest in a member of his family, on March 11:

> "Mr. J. C. Stoney, son of the Rev. J. M. Stoney, has gone into the family grocery business, at Camden, S.C. His many friends here wish him a successful business career."

Regardless of what St. Stephen's might be doing, the Bishop continued to be newsworthy. The issue of April 8th picked up the following from the Augusta News:

> If there is a more eloquent minister in the South than the Episcopal Bishop of Georgia, he does not favor this section with his presence. If there is a more impressive, courtly and eminent representative of the cross in this country his name does not occur to us in the list of the great divines.

A listing on April 15th of the three delegates and three alternates from Christ Church, Macon, also revealed that the diocesan convention would be held in Milledgeville the next month. A longer announcement of the convention followed on April 29th:

> The annual convention of the Episcopal Church of Georgia will meet in this city on Wednesday, May 7, at 11 o'clock a.m. There will be about sixty delegates in attendance, many of whom will arrive on Tuesday, 6th. The convention will be in session two or three days.

Delegates from St. Stephen's were listed as W. W. Lumpkin, T. E. White, and R. W. Roberts.

Meanwhile, on April 22nd, the Rev. Mr. Kimball was reported to have "officiated, using the beautiful and impressive ceremony of the Episcopal Church at the wedding in Sparta of Mr. Henry S. Barkuloo, of Brunswick, and Miss Sallie L. Smith, of Sparta."

The Union-Recorder for May 6 lets us know that St. Stephen's was maintaining a Sunday school and that outside activities were included in the curriculum:

> The Sunday School of St. Stephen's Episcopal Church picnicked at Powell Park on Tuesday last. The day was pretty, and old and young man had a happy time.

That same issue ran a list of both clerical and lay delegates to the convention. It also noted: "The clergy have been assigned homes as follows," though blanks appeared after the names of a few. The bishop's name headed the list, the bishop to stay at the hotel, which was not named. He was to be joined by three other members of the clergy. The names of twenty-three additional clergy were listed. The lay delegates numbered fifty-six. The Union-Recorder did not hesitate to devote space to the convention, or to give high praise to the denomination. One of the several pieces declares, "Few denominations, if any surpasses the Episcopal clergy in learning and personal magnetism." The paper also printed the following notice of appreciation:

> The rector and at the vestry of St. Stephen's Church in this city, would thank the people of Milledgeville for their kindness and hospitality during this session of the Convention held last week.

Just above that that notice appears at the following:

> Thursday, May 15th, being Ascension Day, the celebration of the ascension of our Lord into heaven will be made in St. Stephen's Church, this city at 10 a.m.

In the adjoining column, the editor made note of several persons whom he "had the pleasure of meeting" while "in attendance of the Episcopal convention," one being a former warden at St. Stephen's, Capt. J. W. Wilcox, whom this editor described as "a very valuable man in any city or assembly."

One of the items indicated that St. Luke's in Atlanta had been made the cathedral, though diocesan records contradict the editor. Of course the editor may not have fully understood the meaning of the term "cathedral."

Another paragraph paid tribute to Bishop Beckwith as "not only a grand man in his ministerial position, but no man in Georgia loves to hunt in the woods and pursue the finny tribe in the waters more than he. He is, simply, grand anywhere."

Another delegate was "a Col. Z. D. Harrison of Atlanta, . . . who had spent his boyish good days in this city, and . . . has been Clerk of the Supreme Court for many years." The report on the convention appears under the headline, "THE EPISCOPAL CONVENTION." It begins with the processional hymn and extends for several inches. An offer that would seem to be of great importance to Milledgeville was buried far down in the story. "The citizens of Newnan, Ga.," volunteered "several acres of ground and buildings to establish a female college for the Episcopal denomination." The offer, "referred to the financial committee," is not mentioned in a 1960 history of the church in Georgia.

The usual business of the convention took place. One encouraging report from a "The general Missionary of the Diocese" noted "a marked improvement in collections for missions." It is stated that "each parish through this contributed four missions much more than the assessments." Curiously, the bishop's address was only mentioned, after which is a report of "the election of officers for the ensuing year," including those for "the most important committee," the Standing Committee.

Eight persons were confirmed Thursday night, with the Bishop observing that "there was one female and seven males. It seems that men are taking hold of the faith." He predicted that "the future would show that men as well as women would serve the Lord." (The prelate apparently took no notice of the fact that only men could be ordained as priests at that time.) It to was determined that the next convention would "meet in Christ Church, Savannah, the 10th of May, 1891." St. Stephen's current parishioners believe that "the general sentiment expressed for one of the most pleasant conventions" still holds true, for "the hospitality of Milledgeville is unsurpassed by any city."

No explanation is given on May 13th concerning a ball game, or possibly games, by the cadets at GMC, but because of "the Ball Ground being so near the Episcopal Church as to endanger the building and disturb the services, the cadets and their ball friends of the city are trying to secure other grounds."

On July 29, 1890, the paper carried a correction:

> We were mistaken in stating last week that Sunday night services were held in only one Church in the city during the hot season. Services are held regularly every Sunday night in St. Stephen's Episcopal Church—Rev. W. W. Kimball pastor.

Lay persons at St. Stephen's were called upon to help whenever the rector needed to be away. As noted on August 12th, "On Sunday, the morning service in St. Stephen's Church, was read by Mr. W. W. Lumpkin, the Rector Rev. W. W. Kimball, being absent in Sparta."

On November 4th, the death in Griffin of a Milledgeville native, George Beecher, was reported, with the funeral being conducted in his home town by the Rev. Mr. Kimball. On November 18th, the paper carried a short paragraph under the headline, "IN HOLY BONDS," announcing "At 12 p.m. today in the Episcopal Church, Miss Rosa Mapp, the accomplished daughter of Mr. F. B. Mapp, of this city, will be joined in holy bonds of wedlock to Mr. C. R. Weight of Macon . . . Rev. W. W. Kimball will pronounce the beautiful Episcopal ceremony."

A week later, on November 25th, the Union-Recorder carried the sad news of Bishop Beckwith's death on the 23rd, adding the pronouncement to two paragraphs already devoted to news of his illness:

> Bishop J A W Beckwith was stricken with paralysis Saturday morning, and is lying now in a very critical condition at his house in Atlanta.
>
> Hundreds of friends all over the state, knowing him personally, will be shocked to hear of this; and hundreds of others, loving, the noble character and Christian spirit of the man, will share the sorrow of his friends.
>
> LATER—Bishop Beckworth (sic) died at 6 o'clock Sunday.

For obvious reasons, the Standing Committee of the Diocese "resolved to defer the selection of a new bishop until the next regular Diocesan Convention in 1891" (Malone, 132-33). Fortunately bishops in nearby dioceses assumed episcopal responsibilities for the time being.

Happier news from St. Stephen's made the paper on November 25th with the Mapp-Wright wedding: "At 12:30 p.m. on last Tuesday, Miss Rosa Mapp of this city was happily married to Mr. Randolph Wright. The marriage occurred in the Episcopal Church, the ceremony being performed in well chosen words by Rev. W. W. Kimball."

An account of Bishop Beckwith's funeral, which took place at St. Luke's Cathedral, Atlanta, Wednesday morning at 10 o'clock, appeared in the addition of December 2nd. According to a paragraph on December 9th, "Rev. C. C. Williams, D.D, of Augusta is spoken of in connection with the bishopric of the Episcopal Diocese of Georgia. Rev. Dr. Williams is about fifty-five years of age, and is regarded as one of the ablest divines in the Episcopal Church of the state."

On December 23, there appeared a notice from the Rev. Mr. W. W. Kimball: "Full service, Morning Prayer and Holy Communion, will be held in the Episcopal Church Thursday (Christmas) at 11 o'clock. A cordial invitation extended to all." The "Lenten Notice" was printed on February 10, 1891: "Ash Wednesday service on February 11 to be held at 10:30 a.m.; those on the "Thursday and Friday at 8:30 p.m.," and "Sunday morning—Holy Communion 10 a.m.; Morning Prayer 11 a.m.; Evening Prayer 7:30 p.m." The notice ended with the usual reminder of "A cordial welcome to all."

The obituary for Mr. Henry Perry, a communicant, appeared on February 24:

> Mr. Henry Perry, one of our oldest and best citizens died at
> his residence in this city, on Tuesday afternoon, February
> 17th, 1891 . . . The funeral took place from the residence, at
> 10 o'clock Thursday morning, Rev. W. W. Kimball, of St.

Stephen's Episcopal Church, of which the deceased was a member, officiating.

On March 3rd appeared a notice, signed by the rector, that "Lenten services will be held in St. Stephen's Church every day except Saturday at 3:30 p.m." The same notice appeared the following week. In the issue for March 10, under the heading, "The Society Editor's Week—Chronicle of Personal and Other Gossip," it was noted that "The Rev. W. W. Kimball preached Sparta (sic) last Sunday." Professor Bonner speculates that the Rev. Mr. Kimball "may have also served other churches." One hopes that the sermon did not contribute to a unsavory gossip of the day, listed as it was under the heading of "Personal and other Gossip." The March 10th issue also printed a letter from the rector that Professor Bonner cites as evidence that the Rev. Mr. Kimball's "relations with the local community may have also lacked the resilience which is often required for harmony and good will" (Bonner, *St. S*).

> Mr. Editor:—I learned that it is proposed to have a supper, on the 20th inst., on behalf of the ex-Cadet Reunion. I write to ask would it not be as well to have it after Easter, and it would it not on some accounts be better. The Lenten season closes with Easter Sunday. The Lenten season is, to many, sacred to Holy things. It is commemorative of the fasting and humiliation of our Lord and Savior Jesus Christ. Therefore this is a period of fasting and humiliation with not a few of our city. Sir, I would like to contribute to this worthy object, donations and money. If it is held, as proposed, during Lent I cannot be true to my Savior's memory, and to my Church's teaching and take part in any proposed entertainment. Probably there are many who agree with me in this. So may I ask the committee to postpone the supper until after Easter.
>
> Yours truly,
> W. W. Kimball.

Professor Bonner points out that the rector's "reasons for making this request were entirely valid from a religious point of view and dictated by the tradition of the Episcopal Church in his time and to a certain extent today" (Bonner, *St. S*). The following week, on March 17th, four members of the committee responded, rejecting the rector's request and explaining why, though doing so most respectfully:

> MR. EDITOR: In regard to the card of Rev. W. W. Kimball published in your last issue, this committee beg to say that, while appreciating fully the kindly interest taken in the coming entertainment (Friday night 20th inst.), they can not see how it would be possible to postponement it.
>
> All arrangements have been made for the supper and it would be impossible to get another suitable night for it before the oyster season closes. And besides, this is only one of a series of entertainments that the ex-cadets propose giving before commencement, and to postpone it would seriously interfere with the programme that will follow it.
>
> Trusting that Mr. Kimball and the membership of St. Stephen's Church will aid us as far as is consistent (sic) with their Christian faith and with thanks for their kindly interest, we,
>
> Respectfully,
> D. S. Sanford, C. C. Brantly, R. B. Moore, R. H. Wootten.

After Easter, the ladies of St. Stephen's resumed social activities, according to a paragraph in the Union-Recorder on April 21st: "The ladies up St. Stephen's Episcopal Church will have an entertainment at the Opera House in this city on Tuesday evening made the death."

The following week, on April 28th, readers were urged to support the entertainment in an announcement that also promised "something very unique and novel . . . Look out for program in next week's issue."

> Don't fail to attend the entertainment to be given by the Ladies of St. Stephen's Episcopal Church, next Tuesday night, May the 5th, at the Opera House.

Finally, on May 5th, more information was given:

> The entertainment for the benefit of the Ladies' Aid Society of St. Stephen's Episcopal church will come off at the Opera House this (Tuesday) evening. A pleasing programme has been arranged. Let everybody attend. Admittance 15 cents. The programme begins at 8 o'clock sharp.

Presumably the proceeds would go toward outreach. That same issue carried a single paragraph reminding readers, that "Thursday being Ascension Day, services will be held in St. Stephen's Church at 10 a.m."

A month earlier, on April 7th, the Union-Recorder announced that "the Diocesan Convention which will meet in Savannah on the 13th of May will elect a successor to late Bishop Beckwith." Notice was given on May 12th that "the Episcopal convention of the Diocese of Georgia will meet in Christ Church, Savannah, Wednesday, May 13, and will be in session about three days. The delegates consists (sic) of all of the clergymen of the Diocese and three lay delegates from each parish." No delegates are named for St. Stephen's to what would be the first of three conventions held before a successor to Bishop Beckwith was not only elected, but agreed to serve.

The following week announced the election on the preceding Thursday night of the Rev. Thomas F. Gailor, the Vice Chancellor of the University of the South at Sewanee, Tennessee, "to succeed the lamented Bishop Beckwith."

> The vote was Rev. T. L. Gailor, 17; Rev. C. C. Williams of Augusta, 10; Rev. Alexander C. Garrett, 1.
>
> The new bishop is ranked among the foremost scholars and orators of the South, although comparatively a young

man, having recently passed his thirty-fifth year. He had been profoundly spoken of in this connection, and his election will be no surprise to the diocese.

On June 2nd, the paper reminded readers that "there will be no services in the churches in this city next Sunday. Everybody will go to hear the commencement sermon at college." In the same issue, the first item under a column headed "Editorial Glimpses and Clipping, "made the unqualified statement that "Bishop-elect Gailor will accept the call to the Diocese of Georgia, and will make his home in Atlanta." Curiously, just two days later, on June 4th, the Bishop-elect gave notice that he could not accept the call (Malone, 135). On June 9th, the Union-Recorder reported that "Rev. Mr. Barrett of Atlanta, is pleasantly mentioned in Atlanta as a possible substitute for Mr. Gailor as Bishop of Georgia," and, on the 16th, that a second attempt to elect a Bishop would be made in Macon on Wednesday, July 1.

The name "Beckwith" still struck a responsive chord with the editor, for just above the note on the new bishop appeared a notice that Charles M. Beckwith, a graduate of the University of Georgia, class of 1873 and nephew of the late Bishop Beckwith, had been elected assistant bishop of Texas.

The results of the next election were reported on July 7: "Bishop Ethelbert Talbot, Missionary Bishop of Western Idaho and Wyoming, was elected bishop of Georgia." The newspaper was more cautious in another report in the same issue:

> The new Episcopal Bishop-elect, of Georgia, Bishop Talbot, of Idaho and Wyoming, is about forty years of age, and a Missourian by birth . . . He has not been heard from as to his acceptance, but Mrs. Talbot wants to come and it is a fair presumption that she has some influence with the Bishop.

The paper failed to cite its sources for Mrs. Talbot's feelings, and it was not until September 22nd that the Bishop informed the Georgia Diocese that he was not accepting its call.

Meanwhile, on the Sunday preceding July 14th, "There was no service at the Episcopal Church . . . owing to the illness of the rector, Rev. W. W. Kimball." However, an item in the adjoining column reported that his family was being visited by Miss Carrie Wrigley of Macon. Apparently the rector had not recovered when the funeral of Mrs. Martha Staley, wife of Mr. Joseph Staley, was held at St. Stephen's on the Thursday preceding July 28th, the services being conducted by Rev. Dr. Judd of Macon. Mrs. Staley is described as "a member for many years," and as "another one of Milledgeville old and beloved citizens . . . called away." The next week, on August 4th, appeared a lengthy tribute, concluding with four stanzas of verse, signed by "Ella", who was not further identified. Evidently the rector had recovered sufficiently to travel on his vacation, for on September 1st, the paper carried the following paragraph: "Rev. W. W. Kimball writes that he will return to the city to-day and that services will be held next Sunday in St. Stephen's Church, morning and night." The next week, it was confirmed that "Mr. and Mrs. W. W. Kimball have returned home after a visit of several weeks to Indian Springs and Macon."

Bishop Talbot's refusal to accept the call to the Diocese of Georgia was reported on September 29th: "Bishop Talbot of Wyoming has awarded to the chairman of the committee his formal declination of the Bishopric of Georgia." Readers were being informed of affairs, for on October 13th, the paper ran the following, and misspelled the late bishop's name: "The third Episcopalian convention held this year to select a successor for the late lamented Beckwick (sic) will convene in Macon on the 11th of November." Two weeks later, on October 27th, "Rev. C. C. Williams, of Georgia," was reported as "being prominently mentioned in connection with the bishopric of the Episcopal Diocese of Georgia." On November 3rd, readers were informed that "on Wednesday, November 11, the Diocese of Georgia now must, for a third time, choose a successor to the late lamented Bishop Beckwith." Note that his name was spelled correctly in this piece.

In the adjoining column, "Rev. R. C. Foute, at one time rector

of Christ Church in Savannah during the reign of Bishop Beckwith"
was a reported as being "prominently mentioned" as a successor.
He was currently "Rector of a large and wealthy Church in San
Francisco, Cal." The same issue contained the obituary of William
A. Jarratt, Jr., who died "from a stroke of apoplexy" on the preceding
Thursday. "The only son of Dr. W. A. Jarratt," the deceased was
"37 or 38 years of age. His whole life was spent in this city," and
"his funeral took place from St. Stephen's Episcopal
Church . . . Rev. W. W. Kimball officiating."

On November 10th, the Union-Recorder made the following
accurate prediction:

> In all probability the Rev. C. Kinloch Nelson, D.D., will be
> elected Bishop of the Episcopal Church of Georgia on
> Wednesday next when the Convention will meet at Macon
> Rev. Mr. Hunter and Mr. Z. D. Harrison have visited he M.
> at South Bethlehem, Pa., and they have written the other
> members of the Standing Committee. Mr. Nelson is a native
> Virginian, and Bishop Weed, of Florida, we understand,
> highly endorses him.

In the next report, on November 17th, the paper rather hedged its
bet:

> The Episcopal Diocese convention of Georgia, to eject a
> Bishop to succeed the late lamented Beckwith, met
> Wednesday morning at 10 o'clock, at St. Paul's Church, in
> Macon. Rev. Cleland K. Nelson, called South Bethlehem,
> Pa., was elected bishop . . . But he may not accept the
> position.

The Standing Committee must have been greatly relieved that the
formal acceptance by Bishop Nelson could be reported on
November 24th, though his name was misspelled: "Rev. Clelland
Kemlock Nelson (sic) has formally accepted the call to the bishopric

of the Diocese of Georgia." Also in that issue another outreach project was not only reported but supported by the paper:

> Services of a Thanksgiving will be held in Episcopal Church, Thursday, the 26th, at 11 a.m. The offerings are for the poor. The people of the city are asked to send gifts to the Episcopal Church between 9 and 10 a.m. A committee from each denomination will be appointed to distribute the gifts to the poor of the city. Please send all what you think will do good and will help the poor.

A follow-up appeared on December 1st, under the heading "THANKSGIVING DAY":

> Was very generally observed in the city last Thursday. Nearly all of the business houses were closed, and our streets presented a Sabbath-like appearance. Services were held at the Presbyterian, Baptist and Episcopal churches by their respective pastors. In the latter donations for the poor were received.

The rector himself saw fit to write a more detailed account that also appeared on December 1st. It included a rather unusual gift: three wagon loads of wood. Notice was given the next week that "Bishop-elect Nelson will be consecrated in Atlanta, at St. Luke's Cathedral, on the 25th of January." It is unclear why St. Luke's is again called a cathedral, although, after the Diocese of Atlanta split off from the Diocese of Georgia in 1907, St. Luke's did serve as the bishop's seat for two years (Malone, 140, 149).

After a prolonged period during which no weddings were reported at St. Stephen's, that of Major T. S. Lucas and Miss Olive Herty was duly noted on December 22, with the usual effusions. The same issue announced that "Friday the 25th being Christmas Day, services will be held in Episcopal Church at 11 a.m ... A cordial invitation is extended to all to attend. W. W. Kimball, rector."

The final issue of the Union-Recorder for 1891 appeared on December 29th and carried the following:

> Services were held by the rector, Rev. W. W. Kimball, at St. Stephen's Episcopal Church on Christmas Day at 11 o'clock. The church was beautifully decorated, and the attendance was large.

Apparently, as far as the Union-Recorder was concerned, nothing was amiss at St. Stephen's regarding the rector. Dr. Bonner, however, says that he "appears to have suffered from time to time of poor judgment and lack of perception." Dr. Bonner then quotes from the addition that the Rev. Mr. Kimball made to Mrs. Furman's history:

> I became the Rector January 12, 1890. I found the church in beautiful repair, interior, the Annual Convention of the church [?]. Much good work was done this year for Christ and His Church.

Nevertheless, "early in 1891, troubles began." He blamed "some women, about three," whom he accused of waging "war" and disturbing "the peace of our Zion." He went on to explain that a family named Morris came from New York, from whom the rector asked "letters of good standing from their last parish."

> On the strength of such letters would be forth-coming and presented, I asked the vestry to elect Mr. Rufus Morris a deligate to the convention of 1891.

Unfortunately for the rector, "such letters were never presented . . . I record that Mr. and Mrs. Rufus Morris are not members of St. Stephen's Parish." Professor Bonner explains that "the rector felt obligated to withdraw his own recommendation and to cancel Morris's role as a deligate," adding that this action "offended several women of the parish." The Rev. Mr. Kimball wrote:

> I am thankful to say that all the members of the congregation gave me most loving sympathy and kindly help. Seeing that

kindness would not bring peace, that there was danger of more evil, I resigned January 12th, 1892, to take effect January 31, 1892. I record that the vestry elected 1891 have proven themselves loyal to the Rector and faithful to the church.

He then predicts that "he who succeeds me will have a pleasant and profitable work. I have tried to announce the truest Church principles and I hope the best fruits may grow from them."

Thus ends the year 1891, with apparently no public washing of what might be called dirty linen. However, St. Stephen's would face the coming year once again without a rector.

At least the Diocese finally elected a bishop who accepted the call, though few in his new Diocese could or would attend the consecration at it was first announced. The Union-Recorder noted on January 12, 1892, "Rev. Dr. C. K. Nelson will be consecrated Bishop of the Episcopal Diocese of Georgia on the 25th of January, at his own church, South Bethlehem, Penn."

On January 26th, Milledgeville was notified:

> The Rev. W. W. Kimball will leave on the 1st of next month for Versailles, Ky., where he has accepted a call. His many friends in this city will regret to part with him.

Indeed, the next week's edition confirmed his departure:

> Rev. W. W. Kimball and family left yesterday for Versailles, Ky. Mr. Kimball has been rector of St. Stephen's Episcopal Church in this city for the past two years, and has made many warm friends here who part with him with regret. His call to Kentucky is a desirable one.

In view of what he wrote in Mrs. Furman's history, the outgoing rector did indeed find the move desirable.

On February 16, readers were informed that "Mr. W. W. Lumpkin and family now occupy the rectory of the Episcopal church. We welcome them to the heart of the city."

A follow-up story on the bishop's consecration appeared on March 1st, with apparently the first notice of a change in the place:

> The Rev. Cleland Kimloch Nelson was consecrated bishop
> of Georgia last Wednesday morning at St. Luke's Cathedral,
> in Atlanta. Bishop Charles Todd Quintard was the
> consecrator, and Bishop Howe of South Carolina and Bishop
> Lyman were co-consecrators. Bishop Nelson Rulison of
> Central Pennsylvania preached the consecration sermon.

As might be expected, "the Church was beautifully decorated, and there were present prominent Episcopalians from all over the country. In the evening a reception was tendered for the new bishop and Mrs. Nelson at the governor's mansion." It is interesting to note here little question made about the separation of church and state!

The new bishop's first visit to Milledgeville, scheduled for March 13th, was reported on March 8: "He will preach both morning and evening, and celebrate the Holy Communion at the 11 o'clock service." Even at this late date, apparently not everyone was aware that pews were no longer being rented, for the piece continued, "Pews free. All are cordially invited to attend." The follow-up story appeared on March 15th. One wonders whether a Bishop today would be received as cordially as he was:

> The new bishop, of the Diocese of Georgia, made his first
> visit to Milledgeville last Sunday. He preached in St. Stephen's
> Church at 11 o'clock a.m., and confirmed a class of six.

Our Methodist friends then came to our rescue:

> The Methodist Church, being the largest in the city, was
> rendered the Bishop for evening services. On which occasion
> the eminent divine was given a warm reception by the people
> of Milledgeville without regard to denomination. The church
> was filled to overflowing and chairs and the galleries had to
> be brought into requisition to seat the people.

His sermon was, predictably, praised: "His subject was 'God's love for man.' He preached an able and earnest sermon and made a fine impression on his hearers."

The Union-Recorder for March 29th, contained the obituary for a "Miss Sallie H. Hawkins, an accomplished and greatly beloved teacher in the Middle Georgia Military and Agricultural College . . . of the dreadful disease," pneumonia. "Her funeral took place from St. Stephen's Episcopal Church, of which she was a member . . . Rev. Mr. Judd of Macon officiating."

Strangely enough, on April 19, following Easter, two columns of one page in the Union-Recorder were taken up by what appears to be a complete order of service, including the "Selection and Responsive Reading." It is followed by the texts of "Easter Hallelujah" and "On Wings of Living Light," then two more Easter carols, "Easter Salutation" and "Bright Easter Skies." Services at five churches were covered in a single story. Those at St. Stephen's "were held . . . by Rev. Clarence Lemon of Macon, who preached an excellent sermon." Lengthy descriptions of the decorations were no longer given, simply a judgment that "the church was handsomely decorated. The usual Good Friday services were also held by Rev. Mr. Lemon."

Evidently the search committee had been busy in an attempt to secure a new rector, for the same piece noted: "We learn an effort will be made to secure his services as Rector for this church." Once more the election of members of the vestry was reported: "W. H. Scott, S. W.; R. W. Roberts, J. W.; Jos. Staley, Geo. Barnes, James Barnes and Harry Fox." Sunday School continued in the absence of a rector, according to a sentence on April 26, 1892: "Episcopal Sunday school had a pic nic at Scottsboro last Saturday." On May 3rd, it was reported that "the Methodist, Presbyterian and Baptist Sunday schools have united and will have their annual pic nic at the Park next Friday. The Episcopalians and Catholics have been invited to unite with them."

Instead of the Rev. Mr. Lemon being called, as had been hoped, as of July 5th, "Rev. Charles M. Sturges, from Fernandina, Fla., has written the vestry of St. Stephen's Episcopal Church that he will arrive in Milledgeville Friday, 8th inst. hold services, administer the Holy Eucharist and preach Sunday, 10th July." The piece explains:

> Mr. Sturges is the rector that Bishop Nelson selects for St. Stephen's Church. He comes highly recommended. The pews are free and all are cordially invited to attend. We hope Mr. Sturges will have a warm reception and a large congregation, that he may be induced to accept rectorship of St. Stephen's Church.

On August 30th, the Union-Recorder announced that he had been called and urged "our people" to give him a warm welcome:

> Rev. Charles M. Sturges is expected to arrive on Thursday, the 1st . . . bringing his family, wife and two daughters, who will occupy the Episcopal Rectory. There will be services at St. Stephen's Sunday 11 a.m. The Holy Eucharist will be administered and sermon from the rector. We hope our people will give Mr. Sturges and his family a warm welcome, and give him a full Church next Sunday.

Once more, readers are reminded, "The pews are free, all are cordially invited. Vestry men will be in attendance to show visitors seats."

According to an account in the Union-Recorder, in the absence of a rector, few if any activities had been taking place at St. Stephen's. Readers were informed of the arrival of the new rector and his family:

> On Sunday he was with his Sunday school in the morning, held services, administered the Holy Eucharist and preached to a full house. He invited all Christians to partake of the Holy Communion. He urged the cooperation all the parishioners in his work. In union there was strength and in harmony there was success.

Then followed the editor's evaluation:

> Mr. Sturges has a kind, benevolent countenance affable in
> manner, and genial in feeling. He made a favorable impression
> upon our people. Sunday school and regular services will
> hereafter be held at St. Stephen's Church.

Indeed, the following announcement appeared on September 27th:

> The services at St. Stephen's Church (Episcopal) will be
> until further notice as follows: Sunday school at 9:30 a.m.
> Morning Prayer and service at 10:45 a.m. Evening prayer
> and service at 4:30 p.m." The last sentence again reminds
> readers that "The seats are free and a general and cordial
> invitation extended to all services.

The paper noted on November 29th that "Thanksgiving was very
generally observed in this city," and continued to state that . . .

> Religious services were held in the Baptist Church at 6:30
> and in the Presbyterian, a Episcopal and Methodist churches
> at 11 o'clock a.m. The day was restful and happy to our
> citizens.

With a new rector in place, the ladies once more became active,
according to an announcement on November 29th under the
heading "Episcopal Entertainment": "The ladies of St. Stephen's
Aid Society will give an entertainment on Friday evening, December
2nd, at 8 o'clock." The two-part program, costing 25 cents, was
listed in detail:

> After the performance a substantial supper and refreshments
> will be served by the ladies. This department is under the
> direction of Mrs. duBignon. All contributions can be sent
> to the Opera House on Friday morning.

The observance of Christmas Day was recorded on December 27th with a story on four churches:

> Services were held and all the churches, on Christmas Day
> (last Sunday), and sermons suitable to the occasion delivered.
> Appropriate exercises by the respective Sunday schools were
> carried out . . . The Episcopal Church was beautifully and
> tastefully decorated, and services, conducted by Rev. Mr.
> Sturges were very impressive.

Evidently the new rector was exerting some influence and got the new year off to a good start, for on January 3, 1893, the paper noted:

> The Episcopalian Sunday school gave an entertainment last
> Wednesday evening in the room formerly occupied by the
> bank. The feature of the evening and was a Christmas tree,
> which was heavily laden with presents.

Unfortunately no explanation is given as to the identity of the recipients. Two weeks later, readers were informed that "On last Wednesday, the young ladies of St. Stephen's Episcopal Church served lunch in the store formerly occupied by the Milledgeville bank. The dinner served was well patronized by our citizens. About $40 was realized."

Further evidence of the new life at St. Stephen's occurred on January 29th: "Miss Aurie Brantley has accepted the position of organist at St. Stephen's Episcopal church." It was announced on February 21st that . . .

> Cards or out announcing the approaching marriage of Miss
> Lenora Perry of the city and Mr. Joseph Carthel of Anniston,
> Ala. The ceremony will take place Wednesday afternoon,
> February 22nd, at 2:30 o'clock at St. Stephen's Episcopal
> church.

The follow-up story appeared on February 28th: "St. Stephen's Episcopal Church was the scene of a happy marriage last Wednesday, the occasion being at the wedding of Mr. Joseph Carthel of Anniston, Ala., and Miss Lenora Perry, of this city."

Notice was given on March 7th, under the heading "Bishop Nelson," who would . . .

> visit St. Stephen's Church and parish on Sunday, the 12th inst. The Holy Eucharist will be administered at 7 o'clock, a.m. Morning service at 11 o'clock at which the Bishop will preach and administer the right of confirmation. Evening services at 4 p.m. and sermon from the Bishop.
>
> Extra benches and chairs will be carried to the church, and the vestry will endeavor to seat all, who may desire to come. The pews are free; vestrymen at the door to act as ushers.

The new rector was indeed doing different things, for on March 7th, the paper noted "a robed choir of eighteen or twenty boys, who made their first appearance on Sunday last, who chanted and sang the services beautifully with the regular choir and Rector."

The Union-Recorder did not see fit to name specific churches in its announcement on March 26th that . . .

> Easter Sunday was a bright, balmy spring day. Services were held in all the churches in this city, and the attendance upon divine worship was unusually large. Sweet flowers were tastefully arranged about the chancels, the music was fine and the sermons appropriate to the joyous occasion. The sacrament of the Lord's supper was administered at all the churches.

"The Rev. R. W. Anderson, of Athens, was in this city last week," according to a paragraph on April 11th. "He was rector of St. Stephen's Episcopal Church a few years ago, and has many friends in the city." As a matter of fact, he served in 1884. Two weeks later, on April 25th, readers were told that . . .

> The annual pic nic of the Episcopal Sunday School came off last Saturday at Mrs. F. C. Furman's in Scottsboro. Everything passed off pleasantly, and the children had a fine time.

On May 2nd, the marriage of the next day of Mr. Adolf Joseph and Miss Annie Fox "at St. Stephen's Episcopal Church" was announced.

On May 23rd, the attendance was reported of "Rev. C. M. Sturges, Col. R. W. Roberts and Mr. G. W. Barnes" at "the annual convention of the Diocese of the Episcopal Church at Marietta last week." The paper noted on August 1st that "Bishop Nelson has authorized the establishment of an Episcopal convent in Atlanta and its inauguration is in progress."

The rector evidently had made a very favorable impression on the editor, for on August 29th, the paper reported:

> Rev. Charles M. Sturges has written he will return from his summer vacation on the 29th inst. Services with Holy Communion 11 o'clock Sunday morning next the 3d. prox. And there will also be an evening or night service—time will be announced from the chancel. Choirboys will meet Saturday Sept. 2nd at 3 p.m. for practice.

Then "Our Episcopal friends" were admonished that they "should all turn out and give Mr. Sturges a warm and cordial welcome next Sunday." The editor gave a final urging: "Let there be a full house at St. Stephen's next Sunday."

Another "brilliant wedding" at St. Stephens was reported on September 12th, that of "Dr. R. H. Hutchings, of New York, to Miss Beall Compton of this city, at St. Stephen's Episcopal Church last Wednesday evening at 8 ½ o'clock." The organist for the service, which was described as "one of the prettiest and most brilliant weddings that has taken place in the city in many years," was Miss

Mamie Andrews. "Rev. C. M. Sturges united them in the holy bonds with the beautiful and impressive Episcopal ceremony." Another happy event was reported on November 14th:

> The Episcopalians of this city gave an entertainment at the residence of Mr. J. C. Whitaker, last Friday evening. A pleasant programme of music and recitations had been arranged. Refreshments were served. Those present spent a delightful evening.

On November 28th, readers were told, "Rev. Mr. Judd of St. Paul's Church at Macon preached to a large congregation at the St. Stephen's Church in this city last Sunday. His subject was 'Love,' and his hearers were highly pleased with the sermon." Another paragraph in the same issue reported that he preached "two very interesting sermons . . . Rev. Mr. Sturges filled Mr. Judd's pulpit in Macon the same day." That same issue also announced that "Thanksgiving services will be held at the Presbyterian and Episcopal churches next Thursday. As the pastors of the Methodist and Baptist churches will be absent from the city, there will be no service in their churches."

An announcement on December 3rd of a meeting of the archdeaconry of Macon gives an excellent outline of matters that concerned the church at that time:

> The Archdeaconry, of Macon, will meet in St. Stephen's Church on Tuesday and Wednesday, December 5th and 6th. Bishop Nelson and six or eight clergymen of the Episcopal Church are expected to be present. A first service will be on Tuesday evening at 7:30 'clock, at which the Rev. Mers. Denniston, Damer, and Hunter are expected to make addresses on matters of personal and family religion. On Wednesday morning at 9 o'clock there will be serviced and celebration of the Holy Communion which will be followed by a Conference on the subject of "What it is to be a Churchman?" with addresses by the Rev. Mers. Judd and

Reeves of Macon and the Rev. Mr. Anderson of Griffin. At noon on Wednesday there will be a Literary (sic) Service with special intersession for Missions. This will be followed again by addresses on "Woman's Work in the Church" by the Rev. Mr. Hunter of Columbus, on "The Sunday School, its Helps and Hindrances," by the Rev. Mr. Turner of Hawkinsville.

At 4:00 p.m. Wednesday, the evening prayer will be said, and an address made upon "The Work of the Brotherhood of St. Andrew" by the Rev. Mr. Damer of Macon. This will be followed by an address by Bishop Nelson on "Church music."

At eight o'clock the final service will be held, followed by addresses on Missions by Archdeacon Walton of Atlanta, and others of the clergy.

The people of Milledgeville, irrespective of denominational connections, are cordially invited to attend any and all of these services.

Despite all the detailed planning, some hitches occurred, as reported the following week:

Owing to the unavoidable absence of several of the clergymen, who were appointed to speak at the various sessions, the program as published last week had to be considerably modified as to the order of subjects and the personnel of the speakers, but was carried out entirely as to the times of the sessions.

That same issue of the paper noted:

The Right Rev. C. K. Nelson, Bishop of Georgia, and the Ven. W. M. Walton, Archdeacon of Atlanta, were the guests of the Rev. and Mrs. C. M. Sturges at the Rectory, during the meeting of the Archdeaconry.

> The ladies of St. Stephen's parish entertained Bishop
> Nelson and the clergyman attending the meetings of the
> Archdeaconry of Macon, at a dinner given in their honor at
> the Rectory on Wednesday. It was a neat affair and
> thoroughly enjoyed by all present.

Finally for 1893, a single paragraph on December 26th expressed the regret of the editor "to learn of the illness of Rev. C. M. Sturges."

By March, 1894, the Rev. Mr. Sturges had recovered from his illness, for on the 6th, the Union-Recorder carried a story on the annual meeting of the Baldwin County branch of the American Bible Society, at which he presented one of the "interesting addresses." He was also elected to the executive committee. The next week's issue, on March 13th, noted that he would "visit Sparta to-day and preach to the Episcopal congregation in that city tonight."

A week later, readers were informed, "Daily services will be held at St. Stephen's Episcopal Church, during this week, at 9:30 in the morning and 4 o'clock in the afternoon, except on Wednesday, Good Friday and Saturday. On Wednesday the second service will be held at 7:30 o'clock p.m.; on Good Friday the morning service will begin promptly at 10:30 o'clock, and the afternoon service at 4 o'clock."

Under the heading "EASTER," readers were not treated to the lengthy description of the church noted in former years but only informed that "the Episcopal Church was beautifully and tastefully decorated for Easter, last Sunday." Nor was the sermon quoted, readers simply being told that "at the morning service the Rector . . . preached a very interesting" one. "In the afternoon services were held for the children."

On April 17th, a short paragraph made the startling announcement that "Rev. C. M. Sturges, rector of St. Stephen's Church in this city, has received a call to Augusta. He is an able Minister and has many friends in this city who would be sorry to see him go." Fortunately for St. Stephen's, a week later, under a headline that consisted of only his name, his rejection of the call was reported:

> We are glad to announce that Rev. C. M. Sturges has declined the call to the Church of the Good Shepherd at Augusta and will continue as rector of St. Stephen's Episcopal Church in this city.

He was described as "an earnest and devout worker for the cause of Christ" as well as being "a deep thinker and an eloquent preacher" who "always impresses his hearers. Not only his congregation but all our people will be delighted to learn of his decision to remain here for he is much beloved by our citizens."

The Rev. Mr. Sturges assisted in the funeral for Mrs. W. G. Robinson, who "belonged to an old Milledgeville family," according to a notice on May 1st. "She was ... greatly admired," and had been known "successively as Miss Ann Kenan, Mrs. Saml. T. Beecher, and Mrs. W. G. Robinson."

It was reported on May 8th that "Bishop Nelson paid his annual visit ... last Sunday, and confirmed a class of eleven persons, and preached at St. Stephen's Church ... His address to the class in the morning was listened to by a large congregation." Although it was said to be "full of thought," and to have "made a deep impression on those present," no details were given. The bishop was described as a "fluent speaker" who "has a host of admirers in this city."

On May 22nd, readers were told that "Rev. C. M. Sturges attended the Episcopal Diocese convention at Griffin last week." The rector was still working with the choir boys, for on June 24th, the Union-Recorder noted that "accompanied by the sixteen choir boys of the Episcopal Church," he had gone "down to Mr. Geo. Barnes' place, and spent the week camping out. They had a pleasant time fishing. They returned Saturday. Rev. Mr. Sturges, by his kindness, captured the hearts of little fellows."

The paper kept up with the rector on his vacation. Notice was given on July 31st that Rev. Mr. "Sturges left last Friday to join his family at Turnerville, Habersham county. He be absent from the city until the 1st of September." On August 14th, he was "spending a few weeks at Grand View Hotel, Tallulah Falls." On August 28th, readers were told "Rev. C. M. Sturges and family will return home this week after a pleasant visit to North Georgia."

He obviously did not restrict his teaching to the pulpit, for on October 9th, the community was advised that "the rector of St. Stephen's Church has begun a course of lectures after the Sunday afternoon service upon 'The things which a Christian ought to know.' The first lecture of the course was upon 'Some things about Natural Religions as compared with Christianity.' He next took up 'The Progress of Religious Thought,'" the two serving as an introduction to other lectures on the history of Christianity and the doctrines, order, sacraments, rites and ceremonies of the church." The lectures were not intended only for parishioners:

> A general and cordial invitation is given to these lectures as to all the services of this church. The Sunday morning service begins at 10:45; the afternoon service at 4:30. There is also a service at 4:30 on Friday afternoons.

The Union-Recorder continued to furnish information on the lectures, noting on October 23rd that the next . . .

> will be upon 'The Charges against the Church in reference to [unreadable] and science' . . . and follow immediately after the evening Prayer which begins at four o'clock. There will also be the usual services in the morning on next Sunday, namely Holy Communion at seven and Morning Prayer and [unreadable] at fifteen minutes before eleven o'clock. All are invited to [unreadable] of these services.

On November 13th, his lecture on Westminster Abbey, given "in the chapel of the M.G.N.& A. College last Friday night to the pupils of that institution" was reported. He used what must have been cutting-edge technology, for "it was illustrated by stereoscople (sic) views. There was a large attendance of pupils and citizens who are indebted to Mr. Sturges for a pleasant and profitable evening."

He was still making his trips to Sparta, as noted on November 13th: "Rev. C. M. Sturges goes to Sparta this morning to conduct services in that place tonight."

One of the first mentions of the Daughters of the King appeared in the issue for November 20th, when it was announced that they would "hold a grand bazaar Dec. 11th, 12th, and 13th, when it is expected that there will be an attractive display of fancy work, dolls, dainty crepe and tissue paper combinations, homemade candy, and a plentiful supply of good things to eat." As an added enticement:

> Chocolate will be served by fascinating young ladies, and all who partake of this delicious beverage will have the unusual opportunity of carrying away a dainty cup and saucer as a souvenir.

A week later, readers were advised that "Thanksgiving services will be held in the Episcopal Church next Thursday morning," when a "special offering will be made . . . for the retired ministers of that Church." Further outreach what was planned as well:

> The people are requested to send or bring clothing, groceries, etc., which will be distributed among the deserving poor of the city. The services will commence at 10 o'clock. The public are cordially invited.

The follow-up story on December 4th cover the services in the Baptist and Presbyterian churches as well as St. Stephen's: "Able and appropriate discourses were delivered to large congregations in each of these churches and collections for the poor were taken." No service was held at the Methodist church because of "the absence of the pastor."

Because of its size, readers could hardly miss the reminder on December 11th that "the Daughters of the King of St. Stephen's

Church will give A GRAND BAZAAR in the store next to W. T. Conn Jr., Jewelry store on December 11th, 12th, and 13th." On December 18th, the Union-Recorder reported that the bazaar by:

> the King's Daughters of the Episcopal Church, was a grand success. It was a beautiful and attractive place, and much taste had been displayed by the ladies in making the many things that were offered for sale. Cream and cake, chocolate, etc., were served.

The name of the Daughters of the King was given incorrectly again on January 8, 1895, when the first state convention "ever held in the South" was announced. It was to . . .

> convene in Macon next Thursday, 9th inst. All of our good women who were interested in the good work that has spent and will be done by the King's daughters are invited to attend. The state reformatory question will be discussed and endorsed.

On the 29th of that month appeared in the obituary for Miss Allie L. Hudson, 73, who "died at the home of her sister, Mrs. Margaret Barnes, in Midway, last Saturday night at 7 o'clock . . . She was a member of the Episcopal Church and the funeral services were held at St. Stephen's Church at 11 o'clock yesterday morning, Rev. C. M. Sturges officiating."

The Rev. Mr. Sturges was reported "out again" on February 5th "after a short illness." Two weeks later, on February 19th, "the second of a series of lectures . . . by the Rev. C. M. Sturges" was announced for "the next Thursday evening, at the residence of Dr. T. M. Hall. The subject of the lecture will be 'The Middle Ages and Human Progress.'" The rector was praised as "one of the most intellectual men in our city, and is a pleasant talker. He has given this subject much thought, and will give his hearers a rare literary treat." Another column in that issue explained that "any of our citizens who wish to attend a lecture of Rev. C. M. Sturges can get a ticket if they will call on Prof. D. L. Earnest."

St. Stephen's was certainly brought to the attention of the readers of the Union-Recorder of March 5th, in at least five items. When I took note of the funeral that the Rev. Mr. Sturges had conducted in Sparta the proceeding Tuesday, that of Col. H. A. Clinch. Another item announced "services at St. Stephen's this week on Tuesday, Thursday, and Friday afternoons at four o'clock, and on Wednesday evening at 7:30 o'clock. The last named service will consist chiefly of the Litany and will be followed by an address on 'Abraham, the friend of God.'" The item explained:

> This is the first of a course of lectures to be delivered in connection with these Wednesday night services on the general subject of "Saint—Ancient and Modern." . . . Men are especially invited to attend the services.

Another obituary appeared, that of Miss Adie Whitaker, a student at Georgia Normal and Industrial College: "The funeral services were held at St. Stephen's Episcopal Church, Wednesday morning at 11 o'clock, rector, Rev. C. M. Sturges officiating . . . A fitting tribute to the memory of this lovely girl, from the pen of her pastor, Rev. C. M. Sturges, will be found in another column." Actually, the tribute appeared immediately below the obituary and ran to about the same length.

That same issue also noted:

> Rev. C. M. Sturges delivered the lecture—"The Middle Ages and Human Progress," which he recently read before the "Open Court: To the members of the junior and senior classes." This lecture was prepared with careful thought and study, and is full of information. It was highly appreciated and enjoyed by the young ladies.

Immediately below, the following paragraph on the Bishop was printed:

> Bishop Nelson will visit this city next Sunday. During his stay here, he will be the guest of President and Mrs. Chappell

at the Mansion. He has kindly consented to make a talk to the young ladies, in the study hall of the Dormitory next Sunday afternoon.

Another paragraph expanded on the location:

> The Right Reverend C. K. Nelson, D.D., will visit Milledgeville, and administer the Rite of Confirmation at St. Stephen's Church on next Sunday morning, services beginning at 10:45 o'clock. There will be a celebration of the Holy Communion at 7 o'clock in the morning at which it is expected that the Bishop will be the celebrant. The usual afternoon services will be amended for that day only, because the rector will be accompanying the Bishop to Sparta in the afternoon for the purpose of assisting him in services which will be held there at 7:30 p.m.

That the Bishop did indeed visit President and Mrs. Chappell was confirmed the following week. Further, he had "delivered a most appropriate and forceful lecture to the student of the college," one "listened to with profound attention and delight by the large audience."

No explanation was given in a short paragraph on March 19th as to why "there were no services in the Episcopal and Presbyterian churches" at the "11 clock services Sunday morning." However, it did appear in a paragraph elsewhere in the paper, at least for the Rev. Mr. Sturges. He had "spent Sunday in Atlanta, and preached at St. Luke's Episcopal church." That issue also included a "TRIBUTE OF RESPECT" to Miss Emma Adelaide Whitaker from "St. Agatha's chapter of 'the Daughters of the King,'" a resolution adopted at a meeting on February 28th. The five-paragraph resolution, signed by Ellen Fox, President, and Bessie Furman, Secretary, was printed in full.

St. Stephen's was fortunate the next month, for "the rectory of the Episcopal Church caught fire last Saturday morning from sparks that came out of the chimney and fell on the roof," according to the account on April 9th:

> A reel (sic) house and a fire plug are located near by that Rev. Mr. Sturges, with assistance that happen to be at hand, soon had a stream of water playing on the roof and the fire was extinguished before much damage was done.

That issue also carried a long piece on Holy Week, when services at St. Stephen's would be held . . .

> every morning at 10:00 and every afternoon except Saturday at 15 minutes past 4:00. Friday being Good Friday, there will be three services, the last at 740 P M. The Holy Communion will be celebrated every morning service. On Good Friday morning offerings will be received by the General missionary work of the church. A general invitation is cordially extended to all these services. Those who cannot attend them all are especially urged to be present at those held on Good Friday.
> On Easter Day the services will be at 7:00 a.m., 10:45 a.m., and 4:00 p.m. There will be to celebrations of Holy Communion, when and each morning service, in order that all may have the opportunity to commune on this prince of festivals. At the afternoon service at the summit will be addressed to the children.

The next marriage performed by the Rev. Mr. Sturges was "a quiet home wedding . . . at the residence of Mr. F. B. Mapp, at 9 o'clock Tuesday morning, April 30th. The contracting parties were Mr. C. Irvine Walker, Jr., of Charleston, South Carolina, and Miss Roxanna Mapp of this city."

"Rev. C. M. Sturges and Mr. G. W. Barnes, and Mrs. F. C. Furman and Mrs. Laura Miller," according to the Union-Recorder on May 1st, "attended the 73rd annual convention of the Diocese of Georgia, which met in Atlanta last week." Two weeks later, the impending visit of the assistant bishop of Tennessee was announced:

> There will be services at St. Stephen's Church on next Sunday as follows: Holy Communion at 7:00 a.m. Evening prayer at 5:00 p.m., with a sermon by Bishop Gailor. At this service the Rite of Confirmation will be administered by Bishop Gailor, acting for the Bishop of Georgia.

The piece then explains that "The usual midday service will be held at the G.N.& I. College Hall at 11:00 a.m. at which time and place the annual sermon before the students of the college will be preached by the Rt. Rev. T. F. Gailor, D.D. Assistant Bishop of Tennessee." The follow-up story appeared the following week, as did one of the bishop's sermons at St. Stephen's at 5 o'clock that afternoon. Each item included the usual accolades for the Bishop, "a man of commanding appearance. He spoke without notes . . . After the sermon to the right of confirmation was administered and Mrs. Head and Miss McComb were received into the church."

The edition of June 18th reported that the rector "went on his annual encampment with the choir boys last Wednesday . . . for a week in the woods near the home of Mr. G. W. Barnes."

Although the Union-Recorder told its readers on July 2nd that "Rev. C. M. Sturges left last week for St. Joseph, Mo. and would "be absent from the city nearly two months," he cut his trip short. Apparently he lacked labor leaders to hold services during his absence, for the piece adds that "there will be no services and St. Stephen's Episcopal Church during his absence." On August 6th, however, the paper reported that he would "return to the city this week, and we are requested to give notice that there will be regular morning service in St. Stephen's Church next Sunday the 11th inst. at the usual hour." There followed the usual refrain: "The pews of the church are free and all are invited." His return was confirmed in a paragraph the next week, "from a visit to his old home in Missouri. He preached in eloquent sermon at St. Stephen's Episcopal Church last Sunday morning."

The edition of October 15th printed more happy news involving St. Stephen's, namely the wedding of Miss Elizabeth Furman to Mr. J. Nicholas Tally, of Macon. Miss Furman was "the second daughter of the lamented Farish C. Furman, and granddaughter of the great scientist, Dr. Joseph LeConte of international reputation." The service, conducted by Rev. Mr. Sturges, had taken place at the home of the bride's mother, Mrs. Emma LeConte Furman. Then two weeks later, on October 29th, appeared the unsettling news of the rector's resignation:

> The congregation of St. Stephen's Church or very much surprised on Sunday morning, when Rev. C. M. Sturges, the rector, announced his resignation to go into affect the latter part of November.
>
> Rev. Mr. Sturges has had charge of this parish for three years, and has endeared himself not only to his own membership, but to the entire community, and his resignation is deeply regretted.
>
> Mr. Sturges is a true Christian gentleman, and we wish him Godspeed in his new field of labour. He has accepted a call to Trinity Church St. Augustine, Florida.

On November 19th, readers were advised:

> Rev. C. M. Sturges will preach his last sermon, before going to his new charge, at St. Augustine, Fla., next Sunday at St. Stephen's Episcopal church. It is with much regret that this congregation and our citizens generally part with Mr. Sturges and his estimable family.

The piece adds that "Bishop Nelson has recommended Rev. Mr. Britain of New York to the vestry of this parish, and we learn that he has been called."

Inasmuch as St. Stephens lacked a rector for most of 1896, apparently few newsworthy activities occurred. The ladies, however, carried on with the announcement on January 14, 1896, of "an oyster supper . . . next Friday evening delightful oysters and coffee will be served from 3 to 9. Dainty refreshments will also be served." Readers were admonished: "Let our citizens remember that they can lend assistance to a good cause, and at the same time get an excellent supper. Go and get your supper, and take somebody else with you."

The lack of a rector did not seem to affect the imagination of the parishioners, either. On March 31st, the paper announced:

> Ladies of the Episcopal Church are preparing for an
> entertainment on the evening of April the 10th. This will
> be one of the most unique affairs ever seen in this city. It will
> consist of Living Pictures, Shakespearean Tableaux and a
> baby show. The babies will be a number of young ladies
> dressed as babies.

An announcement the next week about entertainment named specific pictures, and added the information that "an elaborate supper will be served under the direction of Mrs. A. V. duBignon. Admission 25 cents, 15 cents for students of both colleges." Clearly, St. Stephen's wanted to involve the students in parish activities.

Parishioners apparently appreciated the services of a visiting priest, for the same issue reported "large congregations . . . present" when the "Rev. Samuel J. Pinkerton, of Augusta, conducted services at the Episcopal Church in this city, Sunday morning and afternoon. The church was beautifully decorated, and the music was exceptionally good. The Eucharist was administered at the morning services." The Bishop, regardless of who he was, still received attention. The issue for May 26th reported that "Bishop C. K. Nelson has been selected to preach the baccalaureate sermon at the commencement of the State University."

A rector at last! On October 13th, under the heading "ST. STEPHEN'S" came the good news:

> The new rector, Rev. Wiley J. Page, held his first services and
> preached to a full congregation Sunday last . . . The sermon

was a most excellent one and gave general satisfaction to his hearers . . . Mr. Page is the selection of the Bishop for this parish. He comes highly recommended and we understand he will accept the call of the vestry and hereafter morning and evening services will be held regularly every Sunday.

The modern reader can only wonder how long it would be before those readers knew that "the pews of the church are free, ushers and attendance to show visitors seats, and all are cordially invited to attend."

The funeral of O'Hara Foxheld, who died on the Sunday preceding October 27th, was held at St. Stephen's, but no mention is made of the rector. Buried in a long paragraph on December 1st on events of Thanksgiving Day is the information that "services were also held at the Episcopal Church by the rector." Another item gave more details, calling the "learned" rector's sermon a "fine one," and listing the choir members as "Mrs. Rufus Roberts, Mrs. Bland, Miss Fox and Miss Perry."

Wedding bells were ringing for the new rector, as noted on December 8th: "Cards are out announcing the marriage of Rev. W. J. Page of the Episcopal Church of this city, to Miss Margaret Culberson of Atlanta." Two weeks later, on December 15th, the paper told its readers:

Rev. Wiley J. Page was married to Miss Margaret Culberson, at the Church of the Incarnation, Atlanta, Ga., on Wednesday, the 9th inst. The Rev. Albion W. Knight, Dean of the Cathedral, assisted by Rev. J. N. McCormick, Rector of St. Luke's, performed the ceremony. Revs. Wm. M. Walton and Alred Burwell were in the chancel. The music was under the direction of Dr. Cyrill Dadswell organist of the Cathedral, and with his vested choir, the choral service was mostly beautifully rendered.

Then, without bothering to correct the spelling of the names of the bride and groom, "We copy from the Constitution an account of the marriage":

> The wedding of Miss Marguerite (sic) Culberson to Rev.
> Wyile (sic) J. Page at the Church of the Incarnation
> Wednesday night was one of the most brilliant church
> weddings of the season.

The Union-Recorder continued with its own story of the bride and groom's arrival in Milledgeville where they were "met at the depot by Mrs. duBignon with her carriage and driven to the Episcopal Rectory, where a number of ladies of St. Stephen's parish were in waiting. The Rectory house and yards were as neat and nice as possible. An elegant lunch was prepared and served by the ladies. Among the ladies present were Mesdames duBignon, Joseph, Miller, Bland, Lamar and Fenn; and Misses, Thomas, Hopkins, Paine and Miller."

The Bishop was back in the news on February 7, 1897, after giving "an impressive talk to the girls in the Assembly Room of Atkinson Hall on Sunday afternoon." The following week, readers were informed of the illnesses of the pastors of both the Methodist and Baptist churches:

> As the day was pleasant and bright, our people seemed
> anxious to attend divine service, and soon filled the
> Presbyterian and Episcopal churches. Many were unable to
> obtain entrance and were compelled to return home.

Not even the rector was immune to "la grippe," which caused him to be confined to his home . . . last week," as noted on March 2nd.

St. Stephen's rector was still holding services in Sparta, for readers were told on April 13th, "Rev. Wiley Page, of this city, will go over to Sparta this morning and conduct services." They learned on April 20th, in a piece under the heading "Easter services," that "the services at St. Stephen's Episcopal Church were in every way appropriate (sic) beautiful." The piece focused on the music in some detail:

> The choir was composed of Mrs. Marshall Bland, organist, Misses Perry, Woodruff, Mrs. Page, Dr. Manning and Mr. E.E. Bass. The music was perhaps the finest ever heard in the church and was greatly enjoyed by the congregation. Mrs. Bland worked with the zeal and earnestness in having good music and was owing her fine playing and earnest labors to a great extent that the people present had such a spiritual and soul-stirring music.

At this remove, and no one knows why the Bishop chose to deal with divorce in his annual address at the convention at Christ Church, Macon. The Union-Recorder noted on May 11th:

> That portion relating to divorces in the annual address of Bishop C. Kinloch Nelson delivered at the opening of the convention, was the main topic of conversation among the members of the congregation and the people generally after the services.
>
> On the subject of divorce, the Bishop was particularly pronounced that on any other point in the address. He said that the church had no law compelling its Ministers to marry divorced people, and that therefore, it was in the power of the church to refuse to marry them. He warned the clergy of the various parishes that he would expect them to apply to him before marrying any divorced parties, and further born them that he would not sanction any such marriage. "Some bishops," he said, "have taken the ground that such weddings are permissible in our church, but I share no such opinion."
>
> These are radical grounds in the church, and this portion of the bishop's addressed will doubtless cause considerable comment.

It is safe to say that the subject at times still causes "considerable comment." That same edition reported that the rector and his wife "attended the convention of the Episcopal Diocese of Georgia at Macon, last week."

On June 1st, the unhappy news of the death of the Rev. J. M. Stoney was given; no doubt is left as to the high regard he commanded:

> In the death of Rev. J. M. Stoney, which occurred at his upon in Camden, South Carolina, on Wednesday, ninth of May, 1897, a good and useful man has passed away. He had been a sufferer from nervous dyspepsia for some time, and had not been able to preach to his congregation for some months.
>
> Mr. Stoney was well known and greatly beloved in this city. He became rector of St. Stephen's (Episcopal) Church in this place in 1873, and for eleven years was a faithful administered to a devoted congregation. In 1884 he accepted a call to Grace Church, at Camden, where he was the rector for the past thirteen years.
>
> Mr. Stoney was twice married. His first wife died during his residence in this city. His last wife, with several children, survives him.
>
> Mr. Stoney was about fifty years of age. He was an able preacher, a zealous Christian and a sympathetic friend. By his faithfulness to his Master's work, his gentleness and kindness, his loving deeds and kind words, the world has been made better by his having lived in it.

The departure of "Rev. and Mrs. Wiley J. Page . . . yesterday for a visit to Virginia" was reported on July 27th. On September 7th, it was noted:

> Rev. Wiley J. Page, the rector of St. Stephen's Church is expected back this week and there will be service in the Episcopal Church next Sunday morning at 10:45 o'clock a.m. at which service the Holy Eucharist will be administered.

The editor did not hesitate to admonish Mr. Page's flock: "Let the members of the church and congregations turn out next Sunday and give Mr. Page a full congregation." Evidently the date was changed, for on November 23rd, the paper reported:

> Bishop C. K. Nelson, D.D. will preach at the Episcopal Church on next Sunday at 10:45 a.m. and 3:30 p.m. At the morning service he will administered the Lord's supper and from a number of persons. The afternoon service will be especially for the young people, and the ladies of the G.N.& I. College and the cadets of the M.G.M.& A. College are particularly invited to attend. The Bishop will deliver a lecture on 'Travels in Foreign Lands' on Saturday next at 7:30 p.m., in Atkinson Hall. Admission 25 and 15 cts.

The next week, the paper reported that the Bishop did indeed deliver the lecture:

> A fine audience was present, and enjoyed the descriptions of things scene, so vividly and beautifully presented by him. The right of confirmation was administered to four persons and the Lord's supper followed. A large number communed.

That same issue, in a wrap-up story on Thanksgiving, noted that "the services in the Episcopal Church, at 11 o'clock, were very impressive."

The Rev. Mr. page continued his trips to Sparta, holding services "at the Baptist church . . . last Tuesday night," as reported on February 18, 1898. Lenten Services at 4:15 on Mondays, Wednesdays, and Fridays were reported on March 15th, with the Rev. Mr. Page "delivering addresses on the parables," to which all were cordially invited to attend. The editor added his own opinion on the music for the "Sunday service at 11:00 a.m." which he declared to be "greatly improved under the direction of Miss Sterling, aided by a number of her pupils and others." The Easter service was noted on April 12th, but in not nearly the length of earlier years:

> The services at St. Stephen's Episcopal Church on Sunday last were unusually good. The musical program with Miss Sterling as directress and Mrs. Marshal Bland at the organ was exceptionally well rendered from the first to the last number, and the Offertory by Miss Sterling was heartily enjoyed.

The sermon by the rector was termed "strong . . . many communicants remained to partake of the Lord's Supper." It was also noted that "the floral decorations, for which the ladies of the congregation and young ladies of the G.N.& I. College are to be thanked, were the most beautiful seen in Milledgeville in many years." Finally, it was said that "at 4 o'clock the Sunday school held its regular Easter celebration."

Another long story on a regular service debt St. Stephen's appeared on April 26th, where the music again received particular attention. "Full services in the morning" were reported, with the rector preaching. The last paragraph is devoted to the music, which "was finely rendered."

> Mrs. Marshall Bland presided at the organ, and Misses Fox, Sterling, and Mrs. Oertel, with a number of young ladies from the G.N. & I. College, and Messrs. Bass and Oertel composed the choir. The Rector thanked them from the chancel, for the kindness they were rendering the church and congregation of St. Stephen's.

One wonders why suddenly services at St. Stephen's were being given so much attention. On May 10th appeared another story, under the heading "ST. STEPHEN'S," with even more of it devoted to the music in an unusual story about the Rev. Charles Wesley:

> There was a large congregation out last Sunday, the fourth Sunday after Easter. The usual services were held. The rector,

Rev. W. J. Page, preached . . . Mrs. Marshall Bland presided at the organ. The ladies of the choir were Mrs. Dr. J. G. Croley, Misses Fox and Sterling and several of the young ladies of the G.N.& I. College the gentlemen, were Messrs. Oertel, Manning and Richter. The Varrite was chanted [surely "Venite" is intended here], Barrett's "Te Deum," Bragg's "Jubilate," and Mrs. Sarah Adams' hymn of solace, "Nearer My God to Thee" were very finely rendered. As an Offertory Mrs. Dr. Croley and Dr. Manning sang together Charles Wesley's beautiful hymn, "Jesus, Lover of my Soul." It is stated that Mr. Wesley, while in Savannah with his brother John, was sitting by his window when a storm arose and drove a little bird into his room, which sought refuge in his bosom which he kept safely there until the storm was over and the little one liberated. This circumstance, as it is said, suggested the hymn which he wrote, and it has been sung by thousands of Christians ever since.

That same issue announced another of ice cream festival by "The ladies of St. Stephen's Episcopal Church . . . in the Court house square, next Friday afternoon, from 4 to 6:30 o'clock. Everybody invited to come." The follow-up story on May 17th simply reported that the festival had been held.

Bishop Stephen Elliott certainly left a significant impression on the Diocese of Georgia. A memorial to him—an ambitious project "to bring together in family life, with refined surroundings and Christian influences," or to establish a church hall at G.N.& I. College—was reported in the issue of May 24th as having been adopted by "the Episcopal convention in session in Savannah last week." The story was copied "from the proceedings of the convention as published in the Savannah News." The hall would provide "board and lodging" for "20 to 30 girls, whose education will be received in the Georgia Normal and Industrial School, where there is a full corps of competent teachers in all the departments, ample apparatus, etc. Each year finds an increased number of church girls in attendance." Not only would a house mother be put in charge, but also "the priest in charge of St. Stephen's Church at Milledgeville, as ex-officio chaplain. The work of the house would be done chiefly by the girls." Certainly, by today's standards, "the expenses to them would be small, $12.50 to $15.00 a month." Obviously it much thought and preparation had gone into the "long report," presented by its secretary, Mr. W. H. Trezevant:

> The President of the normal and Industrial School has assured the committee of his party cooperation to make the church hall plan a success." necessary funds were itemized as follows:
>
> About $920 for furnishing the hall, and a suitable building can be bought for $2,500 or $3,000, or rented for $25 a month. The income from the fund held by the trustees amounts to about $290 per annum, in addition to which there would be the money received from those accommodations in the fall . . . The Women's Auxiliary will endeavor to raise $900 for furnishing the hall.

The Bishop would continue "as chairman to make further investigations and to take such further steps as may be possible to secure the object desired." Also, "the selection of a house mother would" be his responsibility.

Although the Union-Recorder noted that "Rev. Wiley J. Page and Mr. and Mrs. Rufus Morris attended the 76th annual convention of the Episcopal Church, which convened in Savannah last week," the rector was apparently not interviewed about the proposed church hall. It is not mentioned in a history of the church in Georgia published in 1960.

August 2, 1898, reported that "Rev. and Mrs. Wiley J. Page . . . visiting relatives in Virginia." On the 30th of that month, under the heading "St. Stephen's Church," readers were informed that the rector would "return from his vacation on September 2nd. The services will be held on the first Sunday in September, and will be" at 10:45 a.m., and Sunday school at 9:30 a.m. The piece also explains that "during his absence," the rector had "been in charge of Monumental Church, Richmond, Va. Although he left here for much needed rest and recuperation, (he) has been laboring hard all the time for the Master."

Less than a month later, the ladies were preparing for action again, according to announcement on September 20th that they would "give an ice cream festival on the courthouse lawn on Friday afternoon, Sept. 23, from four to six o'clock. The public are cordially invited to attend."

Regardless of how well affairs seem to be going at St. Stephen's, deaths would occur and remove an active and much lamented member of the parish. "The death of Mr. Frank B. Mapp, about 8 o'clock yesterday morning" was reported on November 8th "as a sad shock to our citizens. He was well known and greatly beloved by the entire community." He had served a number of years has "a Trustee of M.G.M.& A. College." A detailed account of his seizure and a brief biography were given. The funeral would take "place this afternoon, at 3 o'clock, from the Episcopal church." The next week's edition followed up with a story on the funeral, which indeed "was held at St. Stephen's Episcopal Church last Tuesday afternoon at three o'clock, the rector Rev. Wiley J. Page officiating" and reading "the impressive Episcopal burial service."

A short wrap-up story on Thanksgiving, November 29, 1898, observed that the day "was generally observed in this city, nearly all the stores being closed. Services were held in the Episcopal and Baptist churches."

One more funeral remained for St. Stephen's in 1898, though it was not reported in the Union-Recorder until January 3rd, 1899, and it was for a 33 year-old native of Milledgeville, a murder victim:

> Mr. Henry J. Perry, formerly of the city, was shot and killed, in Atlanta, by John Milam, Monday afternoon, Dec. 26th . . . The funeral services were held from the home of Mrs. Perry Wednesday morning at 10 o'clock, Rev. Wiley J. Page, Rector of St. Stephen's Episcopal Church, officiating. The pall-bearers were Dr. Mark Johnston, Messrs. Terrance Treanor, D. S. Sanford, J. A. Horne, H. W. Compton and L. C. Hall.

Even worse news for St. Stephen's appeared in the next week's edition:

> Rev. and Mrs. Wiley J. Page left last Friday for Madison,
> where Mr. Page has accepted the rectorship of the Episcopal
> church. Mr. Page has been rector of St. Stephen's Episcopal
> Church for several years past and has won the esteem of our
> people. He is not only a minister of ability, but is a highly
> cultured gentleman. Milledgeville parts with Mr. and Mrs.
> Page with deep regret.

On January 30th, it seemed Stephen's suffered another loss through the death of Mr. William H. Scott, one of the oldest communicants, described in his obituary on February 7th as "a devoted member of the Episcopal Church" who . . .

> lived a model Christian life. He never knew the taste of
> tobacco or whiskey, and his habits were most
> exemplary . . . The funeral was held at St. Stephen's
> Episcopal Church, in this city, on Tuesday, 31st ult., at 2
> o'clock, p.m., Rev. Mr. Judd, of Macon, officiating.

The paper reported, in two separate paragraphs on February 28th: "At a recent meeting of the members of St. Stephen's Episcopal Church, it was decided not to call a rector, for the present," no reason being given. The second paragraph reported, "Archdeacon Walton, of Atlanta, conducted services at the Episcopal Church in this city Sunday morning. His sermon was greatly enjoyed by the congregation." On March 28th, readers were told, regarding "Easter services," that "Bishop Nelson writes, that he will send the Rev. Mr. Lanier, next Sunday (Easter) to St. Stephens; that the Easter services may be rendered. The Holy Eucharist will be administered. The church will be decorated with flowers, and the music on such occasions is generally the finest."

Apparently the Parish decided it did need a rector, for "the Bishop and vestry are endeavoring to obtain a rector, for Stephen's, and hope soon to have one in charge." As usual, the editor urges,

"Let there be a full congregation Easter," with the usual reminder, "We are authorized to state that the pews are free and all cordially invited to attend." The edition of April 4th confirmed that "Rev. Mr. Lanier preached at the St. Stephen's Episcopal Church in this city Sunday morning. The church was beautifully decorated and the music was very sweet and inspiring. The sermon was an excellent one and was enjoyed by the large congregation present." The same issue noted that "Bishop C. K. Nelson of the Episcopal Church of Georgia will preach the Commencement sermon on Sunday, June 4th, and Gov. A. D. Candler will deliver the diplomas on Graduating Day, with an accompanying address" at G.N.& I. College.

Good news at St. Stephens was printed on April 18th:

> The vestry of St. Stephen's Church and parish, was reorganized shortly after Easter by but some electing Joseph Staley Senior Warden and R. W. Roberts Junior Warden, and Rufus Morris, James Barnes, John G. Thomas and Geo. W. Barnes, Vestrymen. Rufus W. Roberts, Rufus Morris and James Barnes were elected as delegates to the State Diocesan Convention, to be held in Atlanta in May.
>
> The vestry extended a call to Rev. J. J. Lanier, under the approval of the Bishop, who has accepted the same, and assume the charge, preaching his first sermon as rector Sunday last to a full house . . . It was a most beautiful sermon, and well delivered. Mrs. Marshall planned presided at the organ.
>
> Regular services will be held every Sunday. Morning services with sermon, 10:45 a.m.; evening prayer with sermon, 4:30 o'clock p.m.
>
> The pews of the church are free; all are invited. Ushers in attendance to show visitors seats.
>
> The Daughters of the King will hold their meeting at the residence of Mrs. Adolph Joseph, next Wednesday afternoon at 3 o'clock.

Readers were told on May 2nd that "Rev. J. J. Lanier, who was recently chosen at rector of St. Stephen's Episcopal Church has moved his family to this city. Mr. Lanier has been ill since his arrival here." The following week, "services at St. Stephen's Episcopal Church next Sunday" were announced. "The rector, Rev. J. J Kinnear hopes to be well enough to conduct the services, but if he should not be, he will secure the services of another minister." Fortunately, according to the issue of May 16th, he had recovered and "conducted services at the Episcopal church last Sunday. His congregation and friends were glad to see him out again, after an illness of some weeks." The article further reported that the rector and "Judge R. W. Roberts will leave this morning to attend the convention of the Diocese of Georgia, which meets in Atlanta."

The new rector quickly became involved in community affairs. On May 23rd, readers were reminded in the "G.N.& I. College Items":

The commencement sermon will be preached by Bishop C. K. Nelson of the Episcopal Church of Georgia. It goes without saying that it will be a grand discourse. The music for the occasion will also be exceedingly fine, the best voices in the town, both male and female, will make up the choir.

While Governor Candler and Bishop Nelson were "in the city," they were to "be the guests of President and Mrs. Chappell at the Mansion," according to the issue of May 30th. The college column also noted again that the Commencement Sermon would be preached by the Bishop, who would give an address Sunday afternoon, June 5th, to the Young Women's Christian Association. The local Episcopal priest was not forgotten. He was listed in the same edition to give the prayer at the 20th annual commencement at Middle Georgia Military and Agricultural College.

The bishop's "excellent" sermon was given full coverage in the issue of June 6th, when lack of seating space provided an opportunity to campaign for "the erection of an elegant auditorium."

On June 27th, in a column of news from Trilby, it was reported:

Rev. J. J. Lanier visited Mr. James Barnes last week, called on the citizens of the neighborhood. As rector of St. Stephen's

Church at the Milledgeville, this gifted gentleman bids fair
to do good work for the mother church.

The following week's issue noted that "Rev. J. J. Lanier, rector of
St. Stephen's Episcopal Church, conducted services in Eatonton
Sunday." On August 8th, the Union-Recorder reprinted from the
Baldwin Church Record a contribution from the Rev. Mr. Lanier.
Readers were then told that "the Episcopalians of Eatonton have
arranged with Rev. J. J. Lanier for him to preach in Eatonton at 8
p.m. on the first and third Sundays."

On October 3rd, readers were informed that "the young ladies
of St. Stephen's Episcopal Church have proven themselves equal to
any task when it comes to working for the improvement of the
church and rectory." According to the story,

> They recently raised funds for the erection of a front fence
> at the rectory and when it was completed the question
> naturally, arose how could it be painted." naturally, these
> young ladies provided the answer: "Last Saturday morning
> they met at the rectory with paintbrush and bucket and
> went energetically to work. Soon the defense was painted,
> and presented as neat an appearance as if the work had been
> done by an experienced handler of the brush.

The painters undoubtedly appreciated their recognition: "We doff
our hat to the energetic young ladies." Perhaps they worked during
the absence of the rector's wife, for the same issue reported that
"Mrs. J. J. Lanier has returned from a visit to Augusta."

Notice was given on November 28th of a "sumptuous supper
served by the ladies of the Episcopal Church at the opera house
Friday night, Dec. 8th." Elsewhere the same issue contained a
complete announcement:

> The ladies of St. Stephen's Episcopal Church will give a
> unique entertainment at the opera house Friday night,
> December 8th, the programme consisting of a comic farce,

some vocal selections and recitations, together with selections from Miss Laura Paine's Mandolin Class. Immediately following, the ladies will serve a sumptuous supper, consisting of barbecue, Turkey, and salads, oysters and coffee, cake and cream. Their reputation is established; come out and given them a call.

Also on November 28th, it was reported that "Rev. J. J. Lanier has kindly consented to deliver a talk to the members of the Y.M.C.A., at 2:30 o'clock next Sunday afternoon. The men are invited to be present."

✠ ✠ ✠

Then & Now: Almost a century ago, it was decided to close the church in Eatonton to which the Rev. Mr. Lanier once made his visits. The building itself was sold and subsequently used as a private home. The story of All Angels' Church did not end there, however, for in the late 1990s, a group of laypeople living in or neat Eatonton, led by St. Stephen's parishioner and Eatonton Historical Society member James Marshall, approached St. Stephen's then-Interim Rector, the Rev. Roger Ard, about the possibility of holding prayer services in Eatonton. Services soon began, with Evening Prayer often led by Deacon Alice Fay, affectionately known by the Eatonton congregation as "their first angel." Upon the arrival in 1999 of St. Stephen's Rector, the Rev. Dr. C. K. Robertson, the group was ready to move forward with the bold plan of beginning a mission church, actually purchasing the same downtown home that once had been the sanctuary. It was not long before the determination, prayers, and hard work of that original group, now a Steering Committee, resulted in the formation of All Angels' Chapel in the Parish of St. Stephen's. Events then began to move quickly, with the first Eucharist in the newly completed historic sanctuary on Christmas Eve, and soon the consecration of the building by the newly ordained Ninth Bishop of Atlanta, the Rt. Rev. J. Neil Alexander. With the arrival of a newly retired rector from Kenesaw, Georgia, the Rev. Robert Dendtler, the church gained a vicar. Finally, at the Diocesan Council of 2001, this chapel of St. Stephen's gained parish status in its own right. Thus, thanks to the grace of God, the incredible vision and dedication of a small group of faithful laypersons, and the support of the clergy and several members of St. Stephen's, the one-time church— turned house—turned church again became the home of All Angels' Episcopal Parish.

A brief word should be made about the importance of Interim Rectors in key transition points in the life of St. Stephen's. Along with incredibly able lay leaders, interims such as the Revs. Mark ??? and Roger Ard have helped ease the transition after the departure of a rector. At times, an Interim Rector is called on for extraordinary measures. Thus, the Rev. John Buchanon was sent by Seventh Bishop of Atlanta, the Rt. Rev. Judson Child, following a particularly painful time in the life of the parish. Fr. Buchanon did two things in particular that have forever touched or changed the church. The first was to move the Altar out from wall, thereby allowing the priest to face the congregation in worship, a radical, visible change that tied in directly with the new liturgical and ecclesiological emphases of the 1979 Prayer Book. Fr. Buchanon's other major contribution was the hiring of Mrs. Marianne Joris as Parish Secretary, a move for which parishioners since remain deeply grateful.

7

The End of an Era: The 1900s

The ladies got the year 1900 off to a good start when "the Ladies Aid Society of St. Stephen's gave a 'Clipping party,' at the residence of Mrs. Finn, last Friday night," reported on January 30th. The ladies may have given the Friday night entertainments on a regularly scheduled basis, for another was reported on February 27th, this one "at the residence of Mr. Adolf Joseph."

On February 13th came the sad news that "Rev. Henry E. Lucas, who has been rector of St. Mark's Episcopal Church, Brunswick, since 1876, is dead. He was a good man." He had also served St. Stephen's 1872-73. In March, the parish had to deal with the apparent suicide of "a well-known citizen," Richard J. Perry, whose funeral was conducted by the Rev. Mr. Lanier at the residence, though no mention is made it church affiliation.

The Bishop paid his annual visit in April, as reported on April 10th:

> Bishop Nelson, of the Diocese of Georgia, was in the city last Tuesday evening, and conducted services at St. Stephen's Episcopal Church. He administered the rite of confirmation to a class of 10. Those confirmed were: Dr. and Mrs. J. Harris Chappell, Miss Jennie T. Ford, Misses Pauline Brake, Annie Whitfield, Roberta Jarratt, Olive Roberts, Messrs. Stanley Brake, Albert Banks and Leo Joseph.

On May 1st, the Union-Recorder informed readers that "Rev. J. J. Lanier preached at St. Luke's Church in Atlanta on Sunday, April

22nd." The next week, one paragraph revealed that "Rev. J. J. Lanier leaves this morning for Albany to attend the diocesan convention of the Episcopal church."

One of the several items below, reports:

> The vestry of St. Stephen's Church and parish elected Messrs. R. W. Roberts, J. L. Barnes and Rufus Morris to represent the Church and parish in the diocesan convention, to assemble in Albany, Ga., on the 9th inst."

The edition of June 5th carried out the entire sermon by the Rev. Mr. Lanier at the 21st annual commencement of the Middle Georgia Military and Agricultural College. The rector obviously took his vacation in August, for the paper reported on the 28th that "Rev. and Mrs. J. J. Lanier have returned home from a visit to South Carolina." Another paragraph says:

> Rev. J. J. Lanier has returned from his summer outing during which he visited the University of the South at Sewanee. Regular services commence next Sunday. Morning services, with Holy Communion, at 10:45; Sunday School, at 9:30. Let there be a full congregation at St. Stephen's.

Notes from nearby Trilby on September 18th announced that "Rev. J. J. Lanier there will preach here on the fifth Sunday afternoon of this month." The final entry for the year 1900 deals with the observation of Thanksgiving, when "Rev. J. J. Lanier preached an able sermon at St. Stephen's Episcopal Church."

The first event of 1901 was reported on January 22nd:

> On Friday January 25th at 7:30 p.m. Rev. Beverly Tucker, D. D. of Norfolk, Va., representing the Gen. Board of Missions of the Episcopal Church, will preach in St. Stephen's Church, Milledgeville Georgia . . . All are invited next Friday evening 7:00 p.m. at St. Stephen's Church.

On April 2ⁿᵈ, readers were told that the Rev. Mr. Lanier "has been delivering a course of sermons at Trinity Episcopal Church at Columbus, Ga. Rev. Mr. Hunter, the rector of Trinity died at last week. Mr. Lanier remained over Sunday last, hence his absence last Sunday from his church." A report was picked up from a Columbus paper, noting that he had "made a fine impression" before "a large and most appreciative congregation." They were on hand "at Trinity Church last night to hear the second sermon of the series being delivered by Rev. J. J. Lanier, on the Salvation of Man." The Columbus paper, which is not identified, called St. Stephen's rector "a man of unusual force and personal magnetism, and Columbus people are fortunate in hearing so able the minister."

The issue for April 2nd carried the schedule for Holy Week:

> Tuesday, Wednesday, Thursday and Friday at 4 18:00 p.m., and on Good Friday at 10:45 a.m. Sunday next is Easter. Full service at 10:45 a.m., at which time the Holy Eucharist will be administered—The rector and vestry desire as large a collection as possible. The church will be beautifully decorated with flowers. The finest Easter music will be rendered by the choir, which will be assisted by Prof. Fortin. The pews of the church are free and all are cordially invited— Ushers at the door to see visitors.

The full program of music followed. It featured "three violins, played by Mr. Fortin, Mrs. Thomas Lamar and Miss Annie Case; the violin-cello played by Mr. Goodenow, and organ by Miss Lucy Vail (?) . . . The singers are Miss Eva Perry, Mrs. Joseph, Mrs. Callaway, Mrs. Lanier, Dr. Tigner, Mr. Break and Mr. Layfield." The follow-up story the next week, on April 9ᵗʰ, reported:

> St. Stephens was crowded last Sunday to enjoy the beautiful Easter services. Seats had to be brought and, and some had to stand . . . The same program of fine music will be repeated next Sunday.

The following paragraph appeared in another column:

> Rev. J. J Lanier, after holding Easter services at St. Stephen's
> Church Sunday morning in this city, took the 3:45 train to
> fill his appointment to preach at Eatonton night. The
> following members of his Easter Choir accompanied him to
> Eatonton: Mrs. Lanier, Mrs. J. a Callaway, Miss Lucile Vail,
> Miss Eva Perry and Dr. E. A. Tigner.

A piece on April 23rd listed the Rev. Mr. Lanier as chaplain for the Memorial Day celebration, to begin with a parade forming "on Hancock Street in front of the Court House." The follow-up story the next week reported, "Memorial Day was observed in this city with appropriate exercises . . . Rev. J. J Lanier invoked God's blessing." That issue also carried a poem by the rector entitled "Southern Chivalry."

The annual convention received a single sentence on May 14th, with no mention of St. Stephen's. It had "met in Athens last Wednesday, with about 150 delegates in attendance."

Another single sentence sufficed on August 6th to let readers know that the Rev. Mr. "Lanier is visiting Tallulah Falls," perhaps on his vacation, for it was reported on September 3rd that he had returned.

The following week's issue carried the announcement of the marriage "of Miss Annie Lawson Mapp to Captain Fielder Montgomery McGruder Beall, of the Third Infantry, U. S. Army, to be solemnized at St. Stephen's Episcopal Church in this city, at seven o'clock, Thursday evening, September nineteenth." Four paragraphs detailing information about the bride and groom follow. The story of the wedding appeared on September 24th, running to approximately the same league as those of many years ago. The church was described as "beautifully decorated, with palms, ferns and cut flowers, and presented a scene of rare loveliness." All the music was listed, as well as names of the very large bridal party. All in all, it was reported, "the Episcopal marriage ceremony was impressively performed by Rev. J. J., Lanier."

The busy rector was reported on October 1ˢᵗ to have . . .

> left yesterday for a Augusta, where he will be this week and preached on Sunday, at St. Paul's church. On the second Sunday in October he will be in Macon, and the third and fourth Sundays and Savannah. He is away in the interest of his forthcoming book on Biblical Theology, which will be published by Thomas Whitaker, of N.Y., January 1, 1902. While Mr. Lanier is away services will be held in St. Stephen's: on next Sunday, Rev. John F. Porter from Augusta will exchange with Mr. Lanier.

Three weeks later he was reported "in Savannah, where he will spend the remainder of this month." The report continues:

> He is preaching a series of sermons on Biblical (sic) Theology, which he intends to put into book form. We learned that he is quite successful in creating a demand for his book, which will be given to the press the first of next year.

Services were scheduled to be held at St. Stephen's on the Sunday following October 29ᵗʰ. The rector was expected to "return from Savannah tomorrow, and hold services at St. Stephen's Church Sunday morning. Sunday school, at 9:30, and morning prayer, sermon and Holy Communion and 11 o'clock."

Apparently nothing was reported early in 1902 on the book, or any other activities at St. Stephen's until the Easter music was listed on March 25ᵗʰ:

> The Easter services of St. Stephen's will be at eleven o'clock as usual. The music will be rendered by the Choir of the Church, assisted by Mrs. Calloway, Dr. Tigner and Prof. Fortin.

The bishop's visit received a one-sentence notice on April 22ⁿᵈ. He was "expected to visit St. Stephen's Church on May 18ᵗʰ," when he would "administer the rite of confirmation."

Meanwhile, on April 29th, notice was taken of "the series of lectures on 'How We Got Our Bible' being delivered by Rev. J. J Lanier at the Young Men's Christian Association on Sunday afternoons." The editor opined that they "should be heard by every man in the city." The rector's first lecture "so impressed . . . those who heard him that when he attempted to stop, he was kept on his feet some minutes longer by a series of questions." His scheduled service in Eatonton the next Sunday would delay the next lecture until "the week following" when "he will be with the association again."

The obituary of William Jatt, who "died at the home of his mother, Mrs. Roxie Jarrett, in that this city Monday night, the inst., after an illness of several weeks," was printed on May 13th. The Rev. Mr. Lanier conducted the service "at the residence." That same issue reported "Rev. J. J. Lanier is attending the Diocese of Georgia at Augusta this week."

By August 5th, the rector's book had been published, for on that date, the Union-Recorder announced its indebtedness "to Rev. J. J. Lanier for his works, 'Kinship of God and Man,' in two volumes—vol. 1, 'Good and Evil,' and vol. 2 The Master Key.'" The books were hailed as "meeting with wonderful success. The first volume has reached the third edition." The rector was described as "a deep thinker and an able writer, and his books are attracting attention throughout the United States. We learn that they will be republished in England." The same issue noted that the rector "will leave this week for Tennessee, where he will spend a month of August." Upon his return, he was scheduled to give the benediction at the opening exercises of Georgia Military College.

During the week of September 2nd, he was expected to "return from Greenville, Tenn, . . . and will hold services at St. Stephen's Episcopal Church next Sunday morning."

Evidently his writing was keeping him busy. A brief notice on October 14th revealed that he would not accept the office of chaplain of the State Sanitarium, to which he had recently been elected. No reason is given, but the paragraph added that "according to a resolution adopted by the Trustees, several years ago, rotating this position to the ministers of the various denominations in the city, the Minister of the Methodist church will now be named for the position."

A lengthy description headed "Historic Milledgeville" was reprinted "from the *Madison*" in the same issue. Written by Madge Bean McRee, it included six buildings, including St. Stephen's, in a single sentence: "The modern courthouse, and the Methodist, Baptist, Presbyterian, Episcopal, and Catholic churches or all nice, substantial buildings."

The Rev. Mr. Olivier continued his community activity with a series of sermons announced on November 4th, "on 'Church Unity,' St. Stephen's Church, Milledgeville, Ga. Everybody is invited. All the Clergy are asked to take part in the services."

Two items appeared, one under the other, on November 25th. The first noted "Special Thanksgiving services will be held at St. Stephen's Episcopal Church, Thursday morning." The second revealed that "Rev. J. J. Lanier, Chaplain of the Elks, will preach a special sermon to the members of that organization, at St. Stephen's Episcopal Church, and next Sunday morning at 11 o'clock." Finally for 1902, on December 23rd, under "St. Stephen's," notice was given of the Christmas services:

> Next Thursday it will be Xmas, the date that the Church celebrates as the birth of Christ. The ladies meet in St. Stephen's on Wednesday to decorate the church with evergreens. There will be services and sermon at 11 o'clock a.m., at which service the Holy Eucharist will be administered to the faithful. The choir will render fine music, assisted by Prof. Fortin. Let there be a full congregation. Pews free. [Again!] All are invited.

The subject of temperance, to which the Bishop had devoted a good deal of time and thought, provoked "a series of sermons" by the Rev. Mr. Lanier. On February 3, 1903, he was reported to have preached "to a large congregation" on the previous Sunday and "advocated a well regulated dispensary for the county as the next best solution of the whiskey question. He preaches his third sermon next Sunday."

On February 24th, the Union-Recorder printed a long paragraph on Lent and services at St. Stephen's, the contents indicating that readers generally were expected to be Christians but not necessarily knowledgeable about the season.

The approaching season may have prompted the ladies of the church to give "a pleasant entertainment at the Opera House, Friday evening passed." The Union-Recorder reported on February 24th that "A large audience was present, and greatly enjoyed every feature of the entertainment. A nice sum was realized." But the amount was not given.

Evidently the rector's recommendation for a dispensary resulted in a more letters to the editor than the paper could print, for the following appeared immediately above the paragraph on the entertainment:

> The Union-Recorder, at the opening of the dispensary campaign opened its columns to both sides for the discussion of this important question. We were, however, compelled to leave out some well-written articles this week, as the demand on our columns was too great to publish all that was handed us.

On March 10th, the Rev. Mr. Lanier was reported preaching "in Christ Church, Macon, last Sunday and will deliver several lectures there this week." As usual, Holy Week services were ntoed on April 7th:

> There will be services in St. Stephen's Church every afternoon this week at 430 P M, except Friday, which is Good Friday. Piscah or the feast of the Passover, at which feast our savior was crucified, for the redemption of the world.
>
> There will be services in St. Stephen's, Good Friday at 11 o'clock a.m. The altar (sic) will be draped in black.
>
> A committee of the ladies will meet in the Church Saturday morning at 10 o'clock to address the church with flowers for Easter, which is next Sunday.

> The music will be exceedingly fine, Miss Paine at the organ, assisted by Prof. Fortin and Mr. Paul Fortin, together with the regular choir.
>
> The Rector, Rev. J J. Lanier, preaches at morning services, subject, resurrection, after which there will be a celebration of the Holy Communion."

Unbelievably, the last sentence again reported, "The pews are free and all are invited," almost as if the paper used a computer programmed to add that long outdated piece of information whenever services at St. Stephen's words mentioned.

On April 14th, under the heading "Easter Sunday," appeared two items, the first describing the day as "warm and pleasant . . . [but] obscured by clouds which drifted across the skies all day."

> The services in all the churches, at 11 o'clock, were attended by large congregations. Special musical programs had been prepared by the various choirs, and the singing was beautiful and inspiring. The sermons were appropriate and touched on the theme of the resurrection of the Savior of the world. The people entered with thankful hearts into divine worship.

One wonders how many of the services the editor personally attended.

Immediately below, readers were informed, as if it they did not already know, "Sunday last was Easter"; further, they were told that "a large congregation attended St. Stephen's, to enjoy their Easter services. The church was beautifully draped (sic) with flowers; the Rector Rev. J. J. Lanier, delivered one of his finest sermons." The music was praised:

> Miss Paine at the organ, Prof. Fortin and Mr. (sic) Fortin with their violins; together with the regular choir, rendered and the sweetest of music; the congregation joined in the singing. The Holy Communion was celebrated, and a large number communed.

Bishop Nelson was making his usual visits, including one to St. Stephen's reported on May 5th, at which he "preached and confirmed a class of five in St. Stephen's Church of last Tuesday night, 28th ult. The services were largely attended." According to an account on June 9th, the members of the Milledgeville Elks, attending St. Stephen's as a group, "listened to a sermon preached by their chaplain, Rev. J. J. Lanier . . . The Elks made a free will offering of $180.00 to Mr. Lanier."

Undoubtedly, parishioners were gratified to read what the Union-Recorder reported on June 16th, under the headline that proclaimed, "MR. LANIER Will Remain Rector of St. Stephen's Church." He had "determined to remain in Milledgeville" after having "recently received a very flattering offer from the Episcopal Church of Greenville, Tenn., and after giving the subject careful consideration, he determined to retain directorship of St. Stephen's Church in this city. He announced this fact to the vestries last Sunday morning. His decision is highly gratifying to the members of his parish and our citizens generally."

The next month, on the Sunday preceding July 28th, the rector "and family left . . . for a visit to Bay Ridge, L.I. They will be absent from the city until the first of September." Activities evidently slowed during his absence and four weeks after his return, but on November 17th, the paper printed an account of more than one hundred words of the rector's sermons: "Last Sunday, at 23rd after Trinity, St. Stephens had a large congregation, and Rev. J. J. Lanier preached by request, the second time, his sermon on predestination."

The editor declined to "paraphrase any of the sermon," declaring that it "must be heard to be appreciated. Still, he declared that it "ought to be published. The epitome, however, was that predestination is incarnation." Furthermore, "next Sunday he preaches one which follows the connection. Mr. Lanier visits Trilby the first and third Sundays each month, and preaches in the school house to large congregations, and on the last Sunday, a large attendance of Milledgeville people were present."

Notice was given on December 1st that "the Milledgeville Elks will, on next Sunday afternoon, at 2:00, hold a Lodge of Sorrow at the Opera House," The Rev. J. J. Lanier was set to offer a prayer. The same issue noted:

> Thanksgiving Day was generally observed in this city. All business was suspended and the streets had the appearance of Sunday. Services were held at the Episcopal and Presbyterian churches. Large crowds were present, and a spirit of thankfulness pervaded the hearts of all.

The follow-up story on the Elks Lodge of Sorrow appeared on December 8, 1903, under the headline "IMPRESSIVE CEREMONIES." Again, the program was printed, listing the Rev. Mr. Lanier as giving the prayer.

The year 1904 opened on a sad note, with the Rev. Mr. Lanier assisting at the funeral of a four-year-old, Alice Hall Andrews, who died from burns suffered when her clothes ignited from a grass fire that she had set on the lawn of the home of St. Stephen's communicant Adolph Joseph. The story appeared on January 12th.

Undoubtedly, "the friends of Rev. J. J. Lamier are glad to learn that he is convalescing, after an illness of several weeks," according to a short notice on February 16th.

"Services at St. Stephen's During Lent" were noted on February 23rd:

> In addition to the regular services at St. Stephen's on Sundays, there will be evening prayer and lecture on Wednesdays and Fridays at 4:15 p.m. The lectures until further announcement will be on the subject of prayer. These services will be held on Sundays, Wednesdays, and Fridays, rain or shine, so that any one who wishes to come to Church will be sure of having the service.

On the Thursday preceding March 8th, the Rev. Mr. Allen Lanier left "for Pittsburgh, Pa., where he will preach a series of sermons. There will not be any services at St. Stephen's Church until the

23rd of March, when the Lenten services will be resumed, and the subject of 'Prayer' discussed." On March 29th appeared the happy news that the Laniers' son "Richard, who has been desperately ill with pneumonia, has passed the crisis and is now on the road to recovery." Also, in that same issue . . .

> During this week, Holy Week, the services in St. Stephen's Church will be as follows: Every morning at 6:25, Anti-Communion (sic) services.
>
> Wednesday at 4:15 p.m., Evening prayer and an address.
>
> Good Friday, the altar will be draped in mourning. Morning Prayer and Sermon, at 11 a.m.
>
> Easter, the church will be draped with flowers. Morning prayer, sermon and the Holy Communion, at 11 a.m. The following musical programme will be rendered.

The program was printed in full. The follow-up story was on April 5th:

> Easter services and all of our churches last Sunday. St. Stephens was beautifully dreped (sic) with flowers. A full choir rendered sweet music, and the Rev. J. J Lanier, Rector, preached one of his finest sermon sent to a large congregation.

Once more, the vestry election of Easter Monday was reported: "Joseph Staley, Senior Warden; P.J. Fortin, Junior Warden; John G. Thomas, James G. Barnes, and Geo. W. Barnes, Vestrymen." On the Sunday preceding May 3rd, "Rev. J. J. Lanier and Rev. Mr. Northrop, Rector of St. Paul's Episcopal Church, Macon, exchanged pulpits last Sunday. The sermon of Mr. Northrop was greatly enjoyed by the congregation present." On May 31st, the Rev. Mr. Lanier was listed as giving the prayer for the G.N.& I. commencement.

On July 14th, he was reported as "spending several weeks in New York, Boston and several other Northern cities. During his absence from the city regular services will be held at St. Stephen's Church—Sunday school at 9:30 and services at 10:30 a.m." He was back in town in August, for on the 23rd it was reported that "Sunday morning services are held at St. Stephen's Church at 10:30 o'clock. Rev. J.J. Lanier is preaching a series of sermons on prayer."

A week later appeared the obituary for Mrs. Mary Barnes Harrell, of Macon, the wife of Mr. Eli Harrell, whose burial service he also conducted. "Services will be held at St. Stephen's Episcopal Church next Sunday morning at 11 o'clock."

The matter of science and religion apparently had become an issue in Middle Georgia long before it was brought on by the Scopes trial in 1925. A rather bitter exchange of letters ensued between the rector of St. Stephen's and the Presbyterian minister in Monticello, the Rev. Mr. W. Lee Harrell, though the bone of contention was never put in those words. The Rev. Mr. Lanier must have requested permission of the Presbyterian minister in Monticello, to use his church for a series of lectures. Unfortunately, the Rev. Mr. Lee took exception to the theology in parts of Mr. Lanier's book and, according to the rector, began circulating what he called an "UTTERLY FALSE RUMOR, that does me a very great injustice." The Union-Recorder editor saw fit to print on September 27th a lengthy letter from the rector under the headline, "A False Rumor About Mr. Lanier." The rector began by asking, "Will you give me the opportunity of correcting a false rumor, which comes to me in the form of a letter from the Presbyterian Minister in Monticello, who says in answer to a letter from me . . ." There follows the Rev. Mr. W. Lee Harrell's letter, which says, among other things that . . .

> any co-operation with you as to use of church or otherwise in the proposed series of lectures is out of the question. This is due to the subject matter of these lectures viewed as a whole, as set forth in the second Vol. of your book, which has fallen under my eye. There is so much in that book which is unsound and false, that I can give no countenance to its author as a religious teacher.

> I understand that your teachings are discredited by
> your own church, and I thank God there is enough
> soundness in the Protestant Episcopal Church to rebuke a
> priest, whose views are so at variance with the teachings of
> the church universal and the word of God.

Claiming that "in the past" he had "not only extended every courtesy to Episcopal clergymen (some of which they would not reciprocate) but have attended their services, when had the opportunity, and shall do so in the future when I find them standing for the truth. Truth is the bond of fellowship." He signed the letter, "Sincerely, W. Lee Harrell."

The Rev. Mr. Lanier's response, which runs to more than a thousand words, is then printed in the paper. In it, he gives the Presbyterian divine "the right and privilege, if he chooses to think" the rector's teachings "as unsound and false, and my views as being at variance with the church universal and the word of God." But he takes high exception to the accusation that his teachings "are DISCREDITED by his own church." The Rev. Mr. Lanier vehemently denies that his church has ever discredited his teachings . . .

> and as to being REBUKED for my views, Brother Harrell is
> the first person that ever attempted that. If the rumor
> Brother Harrell reports is true, long ago I would have been
> tried for HERESY and DEPOSED from the Ministry of
> the Protestant Episcopal Church. On the contrary, my
> teachings and views have received the endorsement and
> Godspeed of the highest authority in the Episcopal Church.

The Rev. Mr. Lanier then quotes the endorsement of the Rt. Rev. Thomas M. Clark, Presiding Bishop of the Protestant Episcopal Church, who "bought several copies" and declared of the work that "sooner or later it will be likely have a large circulation."

Next, he quotes a letter from "Rt. Rev. Thomas F. Gailor, now Bishop of Tennessee and formally Chancellor of the University of the South," who said of the second volume, "I think it is calculated to do great good and is evidently in the fruit of wide reading and careful thinking." The rector also quotes the bishops of Pennsylvania, Springfield, Texas, and Louisiana: "These are simply a few quotations from many Bishops in the Protestant Episcopal Church, representing all schools of thought—high, low and broad." He asserts that this is . . .

> certainly sufficient to refute the false rumor that my teachings are DISCREDITED in my own church, and that it has me REBUKED me for my views. Nor would I say word about this false rumor, if it did not do me and the Episcopal Church a very great wrong.

September 21, 1904

In the midst of controversy, weddings continued to take place, with that of Martha Auline Brake to Thomas Herty Caraker announced on September 27th, the service to be held at St. Stephen's on October 19th.

The bitter exchange of letters, however, continued in the edition of October 4th, when the Rev. Mr. Harrell based his accusations on the fact that the rector did not quote his own Bishop: "Where is your endorsement from Bishop Nelson? Where is your endorsement from the clergymen of Georgia? I see no endorsement from them in your card relating to our correspondence." Further, the Presbyterian minister asserts that he had heard a "member of the Episcopal Church mention prominent clergymen who do not endorse your views," and offers to conduct the Rev. Mr. Lanier "into the presence of these parties" if he would "do me the honor to call at my residence." He went on to ask if failure of "Bishop Nelson to support your production" doesn't "discredit and rebuke you in effect? . . . When I spoke of you being discredited by the Episcopal Church I had in mind primarily the Episcopal church in Georgia." He censures the rector for not having quoted any clergy from North Carolina and Virginia, where his "contact with Episcopalians has been largely confined to."

There are some outside the church today who might agree with the Rev. Mr. Harrell's assessment that the "impression seems to prevail to some extent that the Episcopal church does not care what its clergymen teach just so they are punctilious as to robe and liturgy, and get up and down at the right time. I have always disputed this impression as an injustice to an estimable body of brethren." He then concedes:

> The array of Bishops whose endorsement you quote goes far toward convincing me that after all my zeal in this matter has been misplaced, and I will fairly promise not to do so any more.

The Presbyterian minister's barrage concludes with a demand that the Rev. Mr. Lanier answer three questions, the first being whether he is "an evolutionist"; the second, whether he believes "in the literal resurrection of the identical bodies of the dead"; and third, whether he believes "in the final salvation of all the human race?"

Of course, that letter prompted a response from the Rev. Mr. Lanier, on October 11th, in which he interprets the Rev. Mr. Harrell's letter as an effort "to convict me of teaching doctrine contrary to that held in Georgia, as if the doctrine of the Episcopal Church was different in Georgia, from that taught elsewhere." He adds that his continued good standing in the national church "is sufficient evidence . . . that I have the endorsement of Bishop Nelson and the clergy of Georgia." He goes on to quote a letter from the Bishop to St. Stephen's: "I trust that the people of Milledgeville will yet enable you to retain Mr. Lanier where his services are appreciated." Although Mr. Lanier says that, as far as he was concerned, "the incident is at an end," he adds a postscript:

> To put the matter of the endorsement of Bishop Nelson and clergy of Georgia forever beyond cavil, I ought to state that volume II was read by Bishop Nelson in manuscript, and

that with his consent and that the of the clergy, I preached
sermons and Augusta, Macon, Columbus, and Savannah,
and secured nearly enough subscriptions to print the first
edition.

The Rev. Mr. Harrell wrote another open letter:

> If Bishop Nelson and the clergymen of Georgia (sic) endorse
> your teachings advertently, that is to say, if they are
> evolutionists idealists, second probationists and universalists,
> all I have to say is that neither Bishop Nelson nor any
> clergymen of Georgia can ever have it for any purpose the
> courtesies of any pulpit with which I am connected.

He then adds, "May God forgive you for trying to sow (sic) broadcast
the stale rationalism of Harvard, and give you a better mind."
    Returning to the rest of life in Milledgeville and the daily
expectations of a rector, the story of the Brake/Caraker wedding
appeared on October 25th, being "solemnized at St. Stephen's
Episcopal Church, in the presence of relatives and a large number
of interested spectators. The church was beautifully decorated for
the occasion," with Mrs. Marshall Bland "at the organ . . . the
impressive ceremony was performed by Rev. J. J. Lanier." That
edition also notes that the rector . . .

> has been granted a three months' leave of absence by the
> congregation of St. Stephen's Episcopal Church, and will
> leave for New York, where he will spend the time preaching
> in the leading churches of that city. He expects to return to
> the city about the first of February.

On November 15th, a Carnival of Nations was announced, to be
held by "the ladies of the Presbyterian, Methodist, Baptist, and
Episcopal churches . . . at the K. P. Hall and Blues' Armory. This
promises to be one of the most interesting entertainments ever

given in the city no date was given." On December 6th, a front-page story reported that the Carnival would be held . . .

> next Thursday and Friday afternoons and evenings, and will be one of the most novel and interesting entertainments ever given in this city. The Methodists as Spain, and the Presbyterians as America, will occupy the Blues', and the Baptists and Episcopalians, representing Japan and the Philippines, will be at the K. P. Hall. The costumes and styles of the various nations will be in evidence, and many interesting features will be put on to make everything pleasant and entertaining.
>
> Tickets are on sale at the drug stores for 50, 35 and 25 cents. A ticket will entitle the holder to visit the two places where the Carnival is in progress as many times as he or she may wish during the two afternoons and evenings, and will give them one lunch.
>
> There is no doubt that anyone visiting the Carnival will get their money's worth, and the ladies are anxious for all our people to come.

Apparently Mrs. Lanier did not accompany her husband on his leave, for on December 6th, it was reported that she would "entertain the members of the Card Club Wednesday afternoon, the 14th inst., instead of tomorrow afternoon." The last notice of 1904, on December 27th, reports:

> Rev. J. J. Lanier has returned from New York, where he has been spending several months. During his visit he preached in the most prominent Episcopal churches of that city. His friends here were glad to welcome him home.

The first notice about St. Stephen's in the Union-Recorder for 1905 appeared on January 3rd and concerned the last event of the previous year, "entertainment last Tuesday at the home of Mr. and Mrs. M. H. Bland at Midway," given by the ladies of the church.

"The little ones had a pleasant time, and enjoyed the trade of good things that was prepared for them."

The rector was listed on January 24th as having given the prayer at the members of the U.C.V., the previous Thursday morning when it members honored "the memory of the Gen. Robert E. Lee." Called upon later, Rev. Mr. Lanier said . . .

> he could add nothing to what had been said by the gentlemen preceding him . . . but illustrating the deep reverence he had for the cause Gen. Lee represented, said his father died fighting for the Confederacy, and had he had a half dozen fathers he would gladly have given them as a sacrifice to his country.

The Laniers also seemed to lead an active social life. The edition of February 7th reported the rector and his wife as having "spent Tuesday of last week with Mrs. J. R. Norment" in Scottsboro.

On February 14th, the Union-Recorder reported that the Bishop . . .

> preached at St. Stephen's Episcopal church Sunday morning [;] on account of the disagreeable weather the congregation was not as large as it would have otherwise been. The discourse was an able wind, and was enjoyed by those present. The Bishop administered the rite of Baptism to one and confirmed a class of three.

Under the heading "EASTER SUNDAY," appeared the following: "Easter services were held and all the churches Sunday morning, and a large congregations were in attendance. The music and decorations at the Sacred Heart Catholic Church and the St. Stephen's Episcopal Church were especially beautiful and inspiring. The sermons were eloquent and appropriate to the occasion."

An item above the Easter story confirmed that the rector of St. Stephen's was continuing to conduct services in Eatonton, having "preached . . . Sunday night to a large congregation. He was accompanied to that city by several of those who sang at the morning service and the same musical program was rendered."

The vestry election was reported on May 2nd after a meeting of the congregation "Monday afternoon" when the following were elected:

> F. G. Grieve, Joseph Staley, J. R. Norment, J. M. Dennis, James L. Barnes, J. G. Thomas and Geo. W. Barnes.
>
> The newly elected vestry met immediately after the meeting of the congregation and elected Joseph Staley, senior warden, J M Dennis, junior warden, F G Grieve, secretary, J. M. Dennis, treasurer, and the following as delegates to the diocesan convention, which will be held in Christ Church, Macon, this month, viz.: J. M. Dennis, Jos. Staley and F. G. Grieve.

Further evidence of the participation of the Laniers in community affairs is given in the edition of May 9th:

> Mrs. J. J. Lanier gave a reception to the seniors of the Georgia Normal and Industrial College last Friday evening . . . The sweet girl graduates presented a most charming picture in their white gowns. The commandant and officers of the cadet corps of the Georgia Military College, in full dress uniform, were present, and completed the picture of beauty and gallantry.

Two weeks later, the paper reported that Mr. and Mrs. J. J. Lanier, along with the lay delegates, "attended the Episcopal convention in Macon last week." There, a momentous decision was reached, the first step in the process to divide the diocese into two separate dioceses, the Diocese of Georgia and the Diocese of Atlanta. However, the Union-Recorder devoted a single sentence to it, in the middle of the report:

> The eighty-third annual convention of the Diocese of Georgia met at Christ Church in Macon, Ga., 17th, 18th,

and 19, of May. St. Stephen's Church, of this city, was represented by Rev. J. J. Lanier, F. G. Grieve and John M. Dennis. The convention was one of the largest and composed of good men. It was decided to divide the Diocese. The colored people of the church were allowed a counsel to themselves, thus separating them from the white convention [a procedure followed until 1947; see Malone 188].

The rector apparently spent the next month, June, away from Milledgeville, for on July 4th, readers were advised that he had "returned to the city from Savannah, where he had spent the past month, and services Friday afternoon and Sunday morning at St. Stephen's Church have been resumed." The next week, the paper ran a resolution from the Women's Guild of St. Stephen's lamenting the death of Miss Etta Miller: Copies of the resolution were to be "published in the city papers, and copies sent to the family." It was signed by Mrs. M. H. Bland, Mrs. Adolph Joseph, Miss Ellen Fox, and Mrs. A. P. Scott, "officers of the guild." No explanation for the change of time for services in Eatonton was given on August 29th, but "services will be held at St. Stephen's Church next Sunday evening at 7:30, instead of in the morning. Rev. J. J. Lanier, the rector, will conduct services in the morning in Eatonton. Announcement as to other services will be made later."

Two weeks later, notice was given of the winter schedule for St. Stephen's: "Sunday school 9:30 a.m. every Sunday; Holy Communion second and fourth Sunday at 11:00 a.m.; on the first Sunday services at 7:30 a.m.; and on other Sundays at 11:00 a.m."

On the Friday preceding November 7th, the rector and his wife were reported to have "entertained the Episcopal students of the Georgian Normal and Industrial College and the Georgia Military College . . . Delicious refreshments were served by Mrs. Adele for 10, Oliver Roberts and genie King." Sometime during the next two weeks, Mr. and Mrs. Lanier visited Savannah, for their return was noted on November 21st.

Finally, on December 26th, the paper noted that the rector and Mrs. Lanier would "entertain the members of St. Stephen's

Episcopal Church Sunday School Thursday afternoon from 2 to 4:00."

Activities in the year 1906 were started by the ladies, whose barbecue dinner was announced on January 9th to be given "on Wednesday and Thursday . . . Dinner will be served from 11 to 3:00."

The next month, on February 6th, the bishop's anticipated visit for the next Sunday was reported. Scheduled to "preach and confirm a class at St. Stephen's Church," he was acclaimed as "one of the ablest pulpit orators in the state, and his sermons are always at masterpieces of rhetoric and diction. Services will be held at 11:00, and the public is invited." Apparently it was no longer necessary to announce that pews were free. It was also noted that the Rev. Mr. Lanier was spending that week "in Hawkinsville . . . attending an archdeaconry meeting of the Episcopal church." Bishop Nelson's visit was reported on February 13th: "He confirmed a class of three, one of whom was Mr. A. C. Westbrooks. The sermon was a masterful one and greatly enjoyed by the large congregation present." Although the war with Spain over Cuba in 1898 seemed not to affect St. Stephen's at the time, Theodore Roosevelt's famous charge up San Juan Hill claimed the life of a prominent communicant of St. Stephen's, A. B. Scott, on January 10th. A "Resolution from a Benevolent Lodge No. 3, F.&A.M., upon the death of brother A. B. Scott" appeared on a February 20th. He was described as having gallantly led "his men in the charge up San Juan Hill in Cuba, during our war with Spain." He died "just as the minister had finished reading the 'committal service of the Episcopal Church,' the reading of it was at brother Scott's request."

Continuing their social activities, the Laniers held "a delightful as well as elaborate party on Wednesday evening to Mr. and Mrs. Jesse L. More," according to the Union-Recorder on February 27th.

An Easter sale by the ladies was announced on April 3rd, the sale to be held "at the drug store at of Mr. Clover and Mr. Kidd, next Friday afternoon, commencing at 2:00. They will have on that sale all kinds of Easter and novelties, aprons, colors, etc."

The obituary of Dr. Coating, "a pharmacist . . . and an officer at the Georgia Sanitarium for years" appeared on April 3rd. Written by Col. F. G. Grieve, long a member of St. Stephen's vestry, Dr. Coating's funeral was "conducted in the Episcopal Church, Rev. J. J. Lanier officiating."

One of the longest obituaries ever printed by the Union-Recorder, appeared on April 10th, announcing the death at his home in Columbus of Dr. J. Harris Chappell, the first president of what is now Georgia College & State University. Dr. Chappell died "last Friday afternoon . . . after an illness extending through three years." The Rev. Mr. Lanier was the first person notified in Milledgeville. A later telegram explained that Dr. Chappell's body "would be brought to Milledgeville for burial, and what a ride in the city Saturday afternoon." The funeral services were held "in the college chapel Sunday morning at 10:00. Rev. J. J. Lanier, rector of St. Stephen's Episcopal Church, assisted by Rev. D. W. Brandon, officiating . . . The beautiful services of the Episcopal Church were read." Dr. Chappell had stood on the rostrum of the chapel "nearly 14 years ago, and organized the College."

The same issue reported on the Easter sale, where the ladies "sold a number of articles . . . neatly and prettily embroidered. A large quantity of candy was also sold. A nice amount was realized," though as usual it was not specified. Holy Week Services were also announced in that edition:

> Services at St. Stephen's Church during this week, which is Holy Week, will be: Tuesday, Wednesday, and Thursday at 6:30 a.m. on Good Friday at 11:00 a.m. next Sunday, which is Easter, there will be Sunday school celebration at 9:38 a.m. Morning Program, on Holy Communion, and sermon at 11:00 a.m. the church will be beautifully dressed in the beautiful Easter music will be rendered by the choir, trained by Mrs. M. H. Bland, the accomplished organist of St. Stephen's church. The public are cordially invited.

The follow-up story appeared the following week. The rector . . .

> preached to the large congregation . . . The Easter music was well rendered by the choir, and the leadership of Mrs. Bland, she presiding at the organ. In the afternoon Mr. Lanier left for Eatonton . . . accompanied by Mrs. Lanier, Miss Snyder, Mrs. Bland, Miss Ellen Fox and Miss Mott . . . for Easter services Sunday night.

A week later, on April 24th, the vestry election was announced:

> The vestry for the ensuing year, that is for Easter Monday, 1906, until Easter Monday, 1907, viz: Joseph Staley, Senior Bordon; and G. Grieve, junior warden. J. R. Norment. Jas. W. Barnhes, J.G. Thomas, G. W. Barnes, Vestrymen. The following were elected as delegates to the next diocesan convention, which meets in Trinity Church Columbus, Ga., May 16th, 1906, viz: F.G. Grieve, J.R. Norment, J.W. Barnes.

On May 8th, the Union-Recorder ran a single paragraph concerning the proposed division of the diocese into two separate dioceses:

> It is thought probable that the Diocese, of the Episcopal Church, of Georgia, will be divided into two Dioceses at the annual convention of the Georgia Episcopalians, which will be held in Columbus, May 15th. Bishop Nelson recommended the division at the last annual meeting on the ground that the . . . large increase in communicants necessitated the change.

The Rev. Mr. Lanier and his wife, along with "Mr. and Mrs. J. L. Barnes, Mrs. M. H. Bland, Mrs. Watt and Anne Scott Whitaker and Colonel F. G. Grieve" were reported on May 10th to be representing "St. Stephen's Episcopal Church at the diocesan convention at Columbus, this week." The next week's edition reported returned from Colombo's of "Rev. J. J. Lanier, Mrs. Lanier, Mrs. Mrs. (sic) M. H. Bland, Mrs. Watt Miss Anne Scott Whitaker and Mr. and Mrs. J. L. Barnes."

Happy marriages continued, with Ms. Bennie wouldn't cent and Mr. Walter of children as being "united in marriage last Wednesday evening at the home of Mrs. Mohr, the bride's mother, on South win streak. The ceremony was performed by Rev. J.J. Lanier," according to the account on July 31st.

The rector evidently took his vacation shortly after the wedding, for the issue of August 28th reported that he would "return Wednesday from Savannah, and will hold services at St. Stephen's Church next Sunday." The return of the rector and his family "from Savannah, where they had been spending several weeks" was confirmed on September 4th.

Two weeks later, another home wedding conducted by the rector was reported, that of "Mr. S. W. Thornton and Miss Lawrence Turk." As if he were not already busy with affairs at St. Stephen's, readers of the September 18th paper learned:

> Rev. J. J. Lanier, the new Prof. of Latin, has entered upon his duties with characteristic energy. Mr. Lanier is an accomplished scholar, and he has the reputation of being a close student. He is a tireless worker and will bring it to his work the consecration of purpose without which success in any calling it is unattainable. It is believed that he will add strength to the faculty.

Regardless of his new duties, the rector and his wife "have opened their home to the public and their friends every Friday night, and will be at home at the rectory to cordially received old friends and who may wish to call," according to a notice on October 9th.

The first announcement of an observance of All Saints' Day was carried on October 30th, to be held "Thursday afternoon at 3:00, at St. Stephen's church. The service will be impressive and beautiful. Everyone invited to attend." Mr. Lanier continued his association with the Elks, giving the prayer for program reported on December

4th. Reminders that the pews were free were still given, as on December 18th, under the heading, "Christmas at St. Stephen's Church":

> The Holy Communion will be celebrated at the morning service, 11:00. The church will be addressed with flowers and greens, client music will be rendered, the rector will preach a Christmas sermon, the pews are free, and every one is cordially invited to attend.

Nobody is safe from the dangers of firecrackers, not even a priest's son. Readers were told a week later:

> Richard, son of Rev. and Mrs. J. J. Lanier, had a narrow escape of being dangerously hurt, Christmas day. He was engaged in popping firecrackers, when a large one bursted (sic) in his hand. Part of the cracker stock camp in the left eye, and it was at first thought that he would lose it. We're glad to learn that he is recovering from the injury.

Easter music at St. Stephen's was listed on March 26th: "Hymn, 109; Christ our Passover, Schilling; Te Deum; Jubilate; Hymn 368; Hymn 488; Communion; Easter morning service 11:00 a.m.; Sunday School service 4:00 o'clock p.m."

The funeral of a Milledgeville native and St. Stephen's communicant Mrs. Laura C. Miller, conducted by the Rev. Mr. Lanier at six Stephen's was reported in that same issue. She had died in New York, where she had lived for two years. The next week's issue contained "IN MEMORIUM," by the rector, for Mrs. Miller. Immediately below it ran the following account of the Easter service at St. Stephen's:

> Sunday was not an ideal day. The weather was cool, it rained during the morning and afternoon, and it grew colder as evening approached, since there was not the crowds out as usual at Easter services, not withstanding all this the altar and chancel where beautifully dressed with white flowers,

some from the garden and some from the wild woods, and with the four new colored glass windows recently placed in St. Stephen's, the Church looked not only pretty but beautiful. The congregation considering the weather was fairly good. The music and singing were sweet and finely rendered, the sermon was one of Rev. J. J. Lanier's best . . . But such a sermon should be heard to be felt and appreciated. In the afternoon, the Sunday School held their services.

The newspaper account may constitute the only record of the installation of the windows, but which ones are not specified. The April 16th edition reported Bishop Nelson's visitation:

Saturday last, Bishop C. K. Nelson administered the rite of confirmation in St. Stephen's church. We understand the six were confirmed. He was assisted by the Rector Rev. J. J. Lanier, and administered the Holy Communion, forty-four communing. A large congregation was in attendance, and the Bishop preached a fine and powerful sermon . . . The Bishop mingled with the congregation after services, and left for Sparta on the 5:00 p.m. train.

One wonders whether the editor really attended the services, despite his description of the sermon, in view of how he stated the number of confirmees.

The diocesan convention was held in Savannah that year, for on May 21st the paper noted, "Rev. and Mrs. J.J. Lanier attended the diocesan convention in Savannah last week," with no mention of the fact that it would be the last convention for St. Stephen's in the Diocese of Georgia.

"There will not be services at St. Stephen's Episcopal Church next Sunday," as noted on June 4th, because the rector would "be in Atlanta, where he will deliver his lecture Ed Dr. Lee and drums Church." His whereabouts were not given in an obituary on June 1st, but Rev. Lamar Semmes had conducted the funeral for Mrs. E eight Richard send at St. Stephen's the previous Monday afternoon.

Picnics were still popular, as seen on July 2nd, for "the members of St. Stephen's Sunday School" gathered for one "at Camp Creek, below the state sanitarium . . . A delightful dinner was served."

A bombshell was dropped in the edition of August 20th, carrying the news of the loss of the rector:

> Rev. J. J. Lanier of St. Stephen's Episcopal Church in this city, has been transferred to Washington, Ga., by Bishop Nelson. Mr. Lanier is one of the most scholarly preachers in the Georgia Diocese, and is a polished and cultural gentlemen. He is a close student and deep thinker, and his sermons are always interesting and instructive.
>
> Mr. Lanier will also serve it churches in Union Point, Madison and other neighboring cities.
>
> Mr. and Mrs. Lanier have many friends here, who will regret to see them leave the city.

The vestry passed a resolution on September 30th, then printed on October 1st, expressing their appreciation to the rector:

> The vestry of St. Stephen's Church met this day and the following preable and resolutions were offered by Mr. Kenan, and unanimously passed:
>
> Whereas our beloved rector, Rev. J.J. Lanier, has accepted a call to God's work in a new field in the Diocese of Georgia, and will on October 1st severed his official connection with this parish,
>
> And, whereas, we feel deeply sensible of his long service to the people of St. Stephen's, and the great sacrifices which have been made by him in serving this parish; and, whereas, in his removal, we and all the people keenly feel a great loss, and entertained the most genuine regret.
>
> Now therefore be it resolved, that this expression of the vestry be made and recorded on the minutes of the church, and a copy of the same transmitted by the secretary to Mr. Lanier, and that our love for the man and are rector, or

appreciation of his noble and faithful work, lofty character, pure and holy purposes be preserved for all time to come.

And resolved further, that the vestry of St. Stephen's Church and parish cheerfully commend him to the most favorable consideration of God.

"Joseph Staley, Senior Warden, Fleming G. Grieve, a junior warden, St. Stephen's Church in Parish, Milledgeville, Ga.

That same issue carried a short notice that "Rev. J. J. Lanier and family will leave Wednesday morning for Washington, Georgia, where they would "make their home. Their friends here part with them with the keenest regret."

They may have left, but on November 5th, Mrs. Lanier was reported to have "spent several days of last week in the city, visiting friends."

On November 1st, the issue of the rector's successor came up:

The congregation of St. Stephen's Episcopal Church in Milledgeville are requested to meet at St. Stephen's Church on Sunday morning next, at 10:00, but the purpose of an important communication from Bishop Nelson, which has been received by the vestry and may be submitted to the congregation . . . It is earnestly desired that there should be a full attendance.

Joseph Staley Senior Warden. F. G. Grieve, Secretary.

And so the parishioners of St. Stephen's, once more without a rector, would march into the new year in a new diocese, the Diocese of Atlanta, created at the convention in May, 1907. They would continue, however, with their old Bishop, who had decided to go with the new Diocese.

✠ ✠ ✠

Then & Now: With the 1907 transformation of a single, unified diocese into two—the urban-based, high-church Diocese of Atlanta and the rural-based, low-church Diocese of Georgia—the relationship of parish to diocese has altered. Milledgeville has moved from antebellum capital to historic college town far from Atlanta. So has St. Stephen's at times appeared to be far from the attention of diocesan officials "inside the perimeter" of one of the nation's busiest metropolitan centers Along with the transformations to both parish and diocese have come vast changes to the Episcopal Church nationwide: Prayer Book and Hymnal revision, the ordination of women, the re-emergence of the order of deacons, and the move to Eucharistic-focused worship.

Thus, we look to an uncertain future . . . but, as the preceding pages remind us, so did our forebears before us. As we pray in the same sanctuary in which they prayed, may we—like they—together find hope in this sacred space amidst the changes and chances of this life.

✧ APPENDIX 1

Rectors of St. Stephen's

Rufus White	1843-1845
William Johnson	1846-1850
George Macauley	1851-1856
? Carmichael	1857-1858
Judson M. Curtis	1859-1861
? Ridley	1863-1864
Benjamin Johnson	1867-1868
John Philson	1870
Henry Lucas	1872-1873
John M. Stoney	1873-1884
R. W. Anderson	1886-1887
H. J. Broadwell	1887-1888
W. W. Kimball	1890-1892
C. M. Sturgis	1892
W. J. Page	1896-1898
J. J. Lanier	1899-1907
W. R. Scarritt	1908-1911
H. L. J. Williams	1912-1913
Clinton Weaver	1914-1915
J. H. Flye	1915-1917
G. Irvine Hiller	1919-1922
Frederick Harriman Harding	1924-1954
William Kirkland	1954-1959

William Littleton	1959-1964
Milton Murray	1964-1970
Jay McLaughlin	1971-1983
Edward Sellers	1983-1998
C. K. Robertson	1999-20??

✧ APPENDIX 2

Twentieth-Century

Wardens of St. Stephen's

Frank Bone	1921-64
Frank C. Davis John P. Thornton	1964
Frank C. Davis Alton Rogers	1965
Frank C. Davis Marshall Bland	1966
John Garner Chester Hodges	1967
John Garner Chester Hodges	1968
Maurice McNabb Joe Hawkins	1969
Joe Hawkins Carter Terrell	1970

Carter Terrell Hugh Cardoza	1971
Perry Moore Hugh Cardoza	July 1971
Perry Moore Jerry Curtis	1972
Perry Moore Jerry Curtis	1973
C. Harold Shadwell Inez Hawkins	1974
Inez Hawkins Carolyn Rotter	1975
Maurice McNabb Carolyn Rotter	1976
Maurice McNabb Walter Bowman Sr.	1977
Perry Moore Jerry Curtis	1978
Perry Moore Inez Hawkins	1979
Perry Moore Maurice McNabb	1980
Perry Moore Maurice McNabb	1981

George Hart   1982
Ken Shermer

George Hart   1983
Ken Shermer

Ken Shermer   1984
Jim Creighton

Jim Creighton   1985
Girlie Sizer

Gene Cornett   1986
Philip Spivey
Jan Hardy

Jan Hardy   1987
Frank Cupitt

Frank Cupitt   1988
Dale van Cantfort

Dale van Cantfort   1989
Chet Helck
Lucy Underwood

Lee Brandt   1990
Jim Simmons

Lee Brandt   1991
Carol Grant

Charles Grimes   1992
Mary Helen Edwards

Tom Blenk Angela Emerson	1993
Tom Blenk Debbie Eason	1994
Debbie Eason Bill Kelly	1995
Bill Kelly Fred Stewart	1996
George Echols Betty Manning	1997
Walt Bowman Jr. Mary Thomas	1998
Walt Bowman Jr. Gordon Stewart	1999
Eustace Palmer Palmer Thomas	2000
Clark Heindel Palmer Thomas	2001
Clark Heindel Jill Roberts	2002
Ken Shermer Dudley Rowe	2003

✧ WORKS CITED

Beeson, Lola. *History: Stories of Milledgeville and Baldwin County.* C. Boyd Publishing Co., 1943. Reprinted Milledgeville, GA: Mary Vincent Memorial Library, 1992.

Bonner, James C. *Milledgeville: George's Antebellum Capital,* Macon, Ga.: Mercer University Press, 1985.

__. *The George's Story.* Second edition. Norman, OK: Harlow Publishing Corp., 1958 (1961).

__. "St. Stephen's Episcopal Church." Milledgeville, GA: St. Stephen's Church.

__. "Sherman and Milledgeville in 1864." *The Journal of Southern History.* August, 1956:269-91.

Coleman, Kenneth, ed. *A History of Georgia.* Athens, GA: The University of Georgia Press, 1977.

Collins, Doris. *The Episcopal Church in Georgia from the Revolutionary War to 1860.* Unpublished master's thesis. Atlanta: Emory University, 1957 (1961).

Cook, Anna Maria Grace. *A History of Baldwin County, Georgia.* Anderson, SC: Keys-Hearn Printing Company, 1925.

Eaton, Clement. *A History of the Southern Confederacy.* New York: The Free Press, 1954.

Encyclopedia Britannica. Chicago: Benton Publishing Co., 1958.

Furman, Emma LeConte. "History of St. Stephen's." Original document. Milledgeville, Ga.: St. Stephen's Church, 1877.

Green, Anna Maria. *Journal of a Milledgeville Girl.* Edited by James C. Bonner. Athens, GA: University of Georgia Libraries, no. 4., ND.

Hinton, Walter Boyd, Jr. "A History of St. James Episcopal Church, Marietta." Privately held, 1957.

Malone, Henry Thompson. *The Episcopal Church in Georgia: 1733-1957.* Atlanta: The Protestant Episcopal Church in the Diocese of Atlanta, 1960.

Morris, Richard C. *Encyclopedia of American History.* New York: Harper & Brothers, 1953.

Thompson, Clara. *Reconstruction in Georgia.* Savannah: The Beehive Press, 1972.

White, George. *Statistics of the State of Georgia.* Savannah: W. Thorne Williams, 1849.

Virginia C. Hinton, a retired journalist and professor, holds an A.B.J. degree and a Ph.D., in English from the University of Georgia and a M.S. in English from Auburn University. Professor Emerita in English at Kennesaw State University, Dr. Hinton also worked several years as a reporter in Atlanta, Cleveland, and Columbus, Georgia. She was a member of the Vestry and Director of Layreaders at St. James' Episcopal Church, Marietta, Georgia, as well as a Vestry member and senior warden at St. Wilfred's, Sarasota, Florida.

Janice A. Hardy holds a B.A. and M.A. from Louisiana State University and is Associate Professor Emerita at Georgia College & State University. She co-authored *Milledgeville, Georgia Methodism* (series), 2003.

Claire Shephard, head of the English Department at Baldwin high School, where she has taught for over 25 years, holds a B.A. and M.A. in English and an Ed.S. in Language Education from the University of Georgia. Along with her husband Todd, she has attended St. Stephen's Episcopal Church since 1975. Currently serving as a Layreader, Mrs. Shephard has in previous years taught Sunday School and been a member of the Choir, Madrigal, Vestry, and Rector's Search Committee.

The Rev. C. K. Robertson holds a M.Div. from Virginia Theological Seminary and a Ph.D. from the University of Durham, England. Rector of St. Stephen's since 1999, Dr. Robertson also serves as Part-time Professor of Communications and Ethics at Georgia College & State University and Adjunct Professor of Pastoral Theology at Virginia Theological Seminary. He has authored or edited several books, including *Religion as*

Entertainment, Religion and Alcohol: Sobering Thoughts, Religion and Sexuality: Compromising Positions, Conflict in Corinth: Redefining the System, and the upcoming *A Capital City: The 2003 Bicentennial Lecture Series on the History of Milledgeville.*